Modern**SUPERBIKES**

Riding the Ultimate Dream Machines

Modern
SUPERBIKES

Mirco De Cet

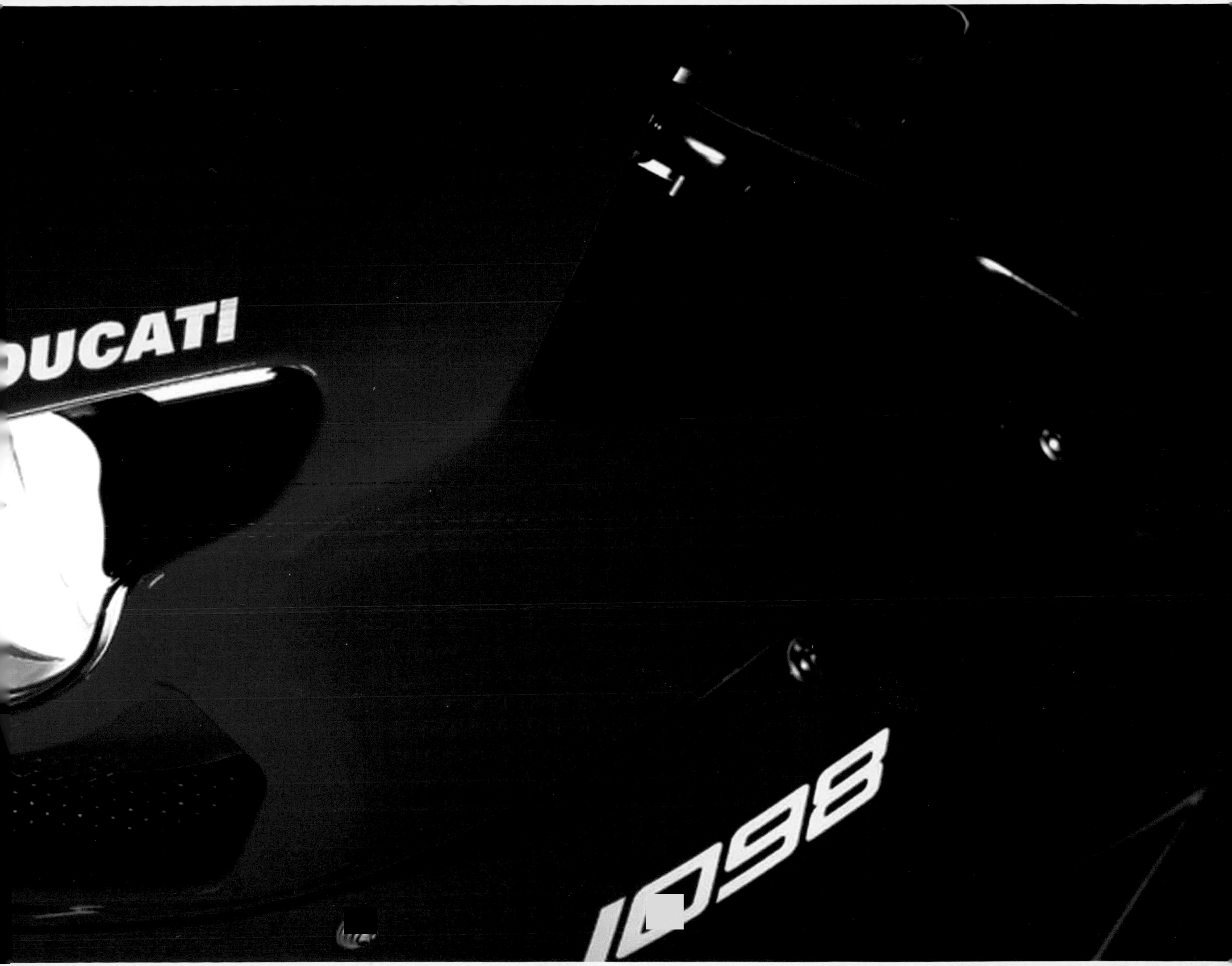
UCATI
1098

This edition printed in 2008

© 2008 Bookmart Limited

ISBN: 978-1-86147-216-8

10 9 8 7 6 5 4 3 2 1

Published by Abbeydale Press
An imprint of Bookmart Limited
Registered Number: 2372865
Trading as Bookmart Limited
Blaby Road, Wigston
Leicestershire LE18 4SE

Produced for Bookmart Limited by:
Editorial Developments,
Edgmond, Shropshire
England

Design by:
Ginger Graphics
Newport, Shropshire
England

Index:
Marie Lorimer
Index Services,
Harrogate, England

Printed in Thailand

Contents

Introduction

The word 'super' is described in the Collins English dictionary as 'a prefix which can be used with many other words to mean above, over or outstanding'. Superpower for example therefore describes something that is extremely powerful. The word Superbike is not in the dictionary, but taking these examples one can only assume that it means a machine of extreme power, a very powerful motorcycle.

With all this in mind and with the title Modern Superbikes, our book has taken a selection of the most exciting motorcycles around today, and given you a blow by blow description of their outstanding features. Most of the machines featured are top of the range production machines that not only reach staggering top speeds, but can also get there in the wink of an eye. We have also included a few others which, although they do not have that 'quick' factor about them, are still fast and furious. I felt these too deserved a mention - after all they are large capacity, powerful, and they do have a very comfortable top speed. Then there are one or two machines that are just outrageously fantastical, which deserve a mention and will only be ridden in your dreams!

I believe that the next decade will see a huge change in motorcycle design and technology. Already the argument about pollution is turning its attention to motorcycles, and sadder still is the constant moaning from the anti-motorcycle lobby, shouting ever harder about motorcycle road accident statistics. Although things will change slowly, change is coming, and personally I smell a whiff of 'no more large capacity' fast motorcycles - there will be no point. So, here we have made a selection of exciting, fast and very hi-tech machines, that I hope will not only give you a pleasurable read today, but in years to come will remind you of these awesome, adrenalin-pumping beauties.

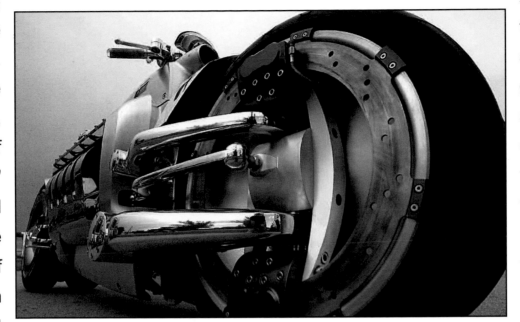

Besides great sex, there will never be anything as pleasurable or exciting as getting your head down behind the tiny screen of a very fast machine, watching the road slip past you as the digits quietly and easily change into the upper reaches of your speedometer. Having to judge corners with pinpoint precision as they come at you at a staggering rate, leaning over to counteract the balance, and then pulling up again to give the machine yet another twist of that all-controlling grip - it's enough to make you want to wet your pants with excitement!

But once you dismount your ride, and the adrenalin stops pumping, the feeling of ultimate satisfaction flows through your body and you are already thinking about recapturing that ultimate feeling, which can only be repeated by another stupendous ride. Ride the ragged edge, but do it in a safe, friendly and sensible manner!

APRILIA RSV1000 R/Factory

Aprilia came about after the Second World War as a bicycle workshop, with its first moped being made in 1962. These early machines, now so very rare, were constructed by three workers, who assembled two per day in a building in the main piazza in Noale, northern Italy - not the birthplace of Aprilia, which was in nearby Scorze.

Ivano Beggio, son of Alberto the founder of the Aprilia company, had a real passion for motocross, and in 1968 assembled a little 50cc machine with the intention of winning the local prestigious race at Giavera del Montello - his ultimate ambition was to become world champion. As in so many cases, the little mopeds paid for the racing, and the racing replicas paid for new development, and so the company progressed. Their motto 'il motore come passione, la passione come motore' - roughly translates into 'the engine as your passion, your passion as your driving force'. Who would have imagined what would be achieved by this little-known company, tucked away just west of Venice!

Left - A shot from the 70th edition of the gruelling Bol d'Or race at Magni Cours, France. The Aprilia Motociclismo Test Team rider Aliverti, gives the RSV plenty of throttle. The team finished 10th overall and third in the Stock category. Right - The RSV Platinum version.

Although in the past few years Aprilia have struggled through some pretty uncertain times, they are now part of the large Italian concern of Piaggio, a highly respected company who are better known for their scooters, and in particular the famous Vespa.

The top of the range Aprilia model and star of the show is the gorgeous RSV 1000 R, of which the 'Factory' version is the outright sports model equipped with lots of 'on-track' goodies. It oozes quality, technology and hi-tech components. Whilst the standard machine is ideal for all the thrills of a track day, the 'Factory' is much more at home in serious competition.

Aprilia is celebrating its impressive sporting record by giving the 200 limited edition RSVs new graphics, which are taken directly from the bike that finished third in the Superstock class at the legendary Bol d'Or - probably the most famous 24-hour motorcycle endurance race in the world.

Left - Taken during the 2006, 24 hour Bol d'Or, an Aprilia Motociclismo Test Team rider tackles the night stage.

Right - The 2007 RSV 1000 R Replica celebrates Aprilia achieving 200 GP World Championship wins. The colours identify Aprilia's triumphant Racing Team over the years.

SPECIFICATIONS

Engine: Magnesium four-stroke longitudinal 60° V twin. Liquid cooling. DOHC - mixed gear/chain drive; four valves per cylinder. Patented Anti Vibration Double Countershaft

Bore x stroke: 97 x 67.5 mm

Displacement: 997.62cc

Fuel system: Integrated electronic engine management system. Indirect multipoint electronic injection. 57 mm throttle bodies

Ignition: Digital electronic ignition, integrated with fuel injection system

Exhaust: Double silencer with three way catalytic converter (Euro 3)

Lubrication: Dry sump with separate oil tank. Oil cooler

Gearbox: Six-speed

Clutch: Multi-plate. Metal braided clutch line

Primary drive: Spur gears

Final drive: Chain

Frame: Box section sloping twin-spar in aluminium alloy

Front suspension: 43 mm Öhlins titanium nitride (TiN) coated upside-down fork

Rear suspension: Aluminium alloy double arched member swingarm with Sachs monoshock

Brakes Brembo

Front: Double stainless steel floating disc - 320 mm. Radial callipers with four 34 mm pistons and four sintered pads

Rear: Stainless steel disc - 220 mm. Twin 32 mm piston calliper. Sintered pads

Wheels Aluminium alloy

Front: 3.50 x 17 in

Rear: 6.00 x 17 in

Tyres Radial tubeless

Front: 120/70 ZR 17

Rear: 190/50 ZR 17

Overall length: 2,035 mm

Overall width: 730 mm (at handlebars)

Overall height: 1,130 mm (at windshield)

Seat height: 810 mm

Wheelbase: 1,418 mm

Dry weight: 189 kg,

Tank capacity: 18 litres, 4 litre reserve

The Öhlins racing monoshock fitted to the Factory model, is not only adjustable in preload, compression and extension but in length also.

V60 MAGNESIUM ENGINE

The 1000cc V60 Magnesium engine has long been the standard setter for production twins, but constant evolution and development at Aprilia's R&D department have now made it even better - 33 mm exhaust valves and new, larger diameter exhaust headers have been fitted to improve engine breathing. In this form the V60 Magnesium now puts out even more power, topping 143 hp at 10,000 rpm without losing any of its legendary usability and reliability.

The air scoop located in the nose of the fairing has been redesigned to increase air-flow to the engine.

A simple to read tachometer and digital speed indicator, with warning lights to the left of the housing.

Satin finish, stainless steel silencers have catalytic converters positioned as near to the collector pipe as possible to enhance engine efficiency.

APRILIA TUONO
Factory

Alongside the RSV100R in the Aprilia stable is the new and exciting Tuono 1000 R 'Factory'. For those who appreciate exclusive design, top build quality and who want to extract maximum pleasure and satisfaction from their ride, this amazing machine ranks amongst the world's most competitive naked bikes.

The performance of the Tuono 1000 R Factory has been boosted to the maximum with the adoption of the same latest generation engine that powers the incredible RSV 1000 R Factory. Even more sophisticated chassis enhancements give the bike exceptional dynamics, and allow you to ride like a true professional not only on the road but on the track too. This is a machine itching to get you on the road!

SPECIFICATION

Engine:	Magnesium. Longitudinal 60° V-twin, four-stroke. Liquid cooling DOHC, 4VPC. Patented AVDC anti-vibration double countershaft.	**Brakes**	Brembo
		Front:	Double floating disc in stainless steel - 320 mm Brembo radial callipers with four 34 mm pistons and four sintered pads. Metal braided brake hose
Bore x stroke:	97 x 67.5 mm		
Displacement:	997.62cc		
Fuel system:	Integrated electronic engine management system. Indirect multi-point electronic fuel injection. 57 mm diameter throttle bodies	**Rear:**	Stainless steel disc - 220 mm. Single calliper with two 32 mm pistons and sintered pads. Metal braided brake hose
		Wheels:	Aluminium alloy
Ignition:	Digital electronic ignition, integrated with the fuel injection system	**Front:**	3.50 x 17 in
		Rear:	6.00 x 17 in
Exhaust system:	Two silencers with three-way catalytic converter (Euro 3)	**Tyres:**	Radial tubeless
		Front:	120/70 ZR 17
Lubrication:	Dry sump with separate oil reservoir. Oil cooler	**Rear:**	180/55 ZR 17
		Overall length:	2,025 mm
Gearbox:	Six-speed	**Overall width:**	830 mm (at handlebars)
Clutch:	Multiple disc in oil bath with patented PPC power-assisted hydraulic control. Metal braided clutch hose	**Overall height:**	1,100 mm (at handlebars)
		Seat height:	810 mm
		Wheelbase:	1,410 mm
Primary drive:	Spur gears	**Dry weight:**	181 kg dry
Final drive:	Chain	**Tank capacity:**	18 litres, 4 litre reserve
Frame:	Box section sloping twin-spar frame in aluminiumalloy		
Front suspension:	Öhlins Racing 43mm upside-down fork		
Rear suspension:	Aluminium alloy double member swingarm. APS (Aprilia Progressive System) rising rate linkages. Öhlins Racing piggy-back monoshock		

BENELLI Tornado Tre 1130

There is nothing like the resurrection of an old-established company to create excitement and gossip. When word filtered down that Benelli were going to introduce their first motorcycle for some twenty years or so, the gossip scale went through the roof as all sorts of rumours started to flow.

From the initial rumours, there was quite some time before anything did in fact happen, but when it did, it was out of the ordinary - well, I guess it had to be really. The resultant presentation was the Benelli Tornado Tre superbike, and that was back in 2002. Today Benelli have a small but interesting range of machines; the Tornado Tre 1130 is a further development of that original machine and has all its qualities and more.

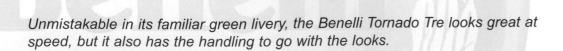

Unmistakable in its familiar green livery, the Benelli Tornado Tre looks great at speed, but it also has the handling to go with the looks.

After some turbulent years and the disappearance of the company name from the motorcycling scene after the 1970s, Benelli came back with a vengeance. They have some stunning looking machinery and the Tornado Tre 1130 is just one.

The lines of the 1130 speak for themselves - this is a sports bike that would probably feel more at home on the track rather than on the normal road. Don't be fooled though, as it will handle everyday open riding with ease and comfort. The machine has all the sophistication that Benelli bring with racing expertise gained over many years. The 1130 is a powerful machine equipped with all the modern technological advantages, that will make any rider appreciate this stunningly well behaved machine.

The 1130 has been restyled and differs from the original Tre, becoming exclusive in its own way. For example the frame, swingarm and steering plate have been painted black, helping to give the overall appearance of compactness and streamlining, but at the same time keeping a tight grip on its heritage.

The grey and black paint scheme shows the machine off well. Under the rear cowling the two hot air extractor vents can be easily spotted.

The Tornado Tre 1130 engine:

The 1130cc, three-cylinder, in-line engine, is even more powerful and has better performance in this version. The profile of the cams and the intake runners have been changed, making engine operation smoother and more powerful. The injection control unit software has also been optimised for an improved ride on the track, and constant performance is enhanced by the addition of the oil cooling system which includes a radiator. There is a fully removable six-speed gearbox which, as on all competition bikes, allows rapid gear substitution without taking the engine to bits.

SPECIFICATION

Engine:	Four-stroke, DOHC, 4VPC, Three-cylinder in-line, tilted forward 15°, with anti-vibration countershaft
Bore x stroke:	88 x 62 mm
Displacement:	1130cc
Ignition:	Single coil inductive discharge electronic ignition Electronic injection
Lubrication:	Wet sump
Cooling system:	Water with rear-mounted radiator and two electric cooling fans
Oil cooling system:	Radiator
Gearbox:	Six-speed
Clutch:	Dry
Transmission:	Straight toothed primary gear, chain-driven secondary
Frame:	Front trusses in ASD tubular steel securely fitted with traction screws, with aluminium alloy casting rear section
Front suspension:	Marzocchi upside-down stanchion fork Ø 50 mm
Rear suspension:	Asymmetric swingarm, composed of cast aluminium and pressed in aluminium alloy, with 'Extreme Technology' single shock absorber
Brakes:	Brembo
Front:	Double floating disc - 320 mm. Four-piston callipers
Rear:	Single disc - 240 mm. Twin-piston calliper
Wheels:	Brembo die-cast aluminium alloy
Front:	3.5 x 17 in
Rear:	6.00 x 17 in
Tyres:	Tubeless radial
Front:	120/70 x 17 in
Rear:	190/50 x 17 in
Wheelbase:	1419 mm
Seat height:	810 mm

Glowing as if they were some nuclear danger zone, these are the two grated outlets for the excess hot air from the engine.

Enough instrumentation to let you know where the danger zones are, and a damper to assist you on those twisty bits.

A fast machine needs to be equipped with a good braking system. Seen here is the rear brake disc and Brembo calliper.

BENELLI TNT 1130 Sport

You could say that the TNT is a radical looking machine, but styling-wise it is the norm for a naked bike these days. It is one of a number that have this rather aggressive, praying mantis-like feature.

Benelli say that the TNT Sport is inspired by the superbike motorcycles aimed at the most enthusiastic sports riders. It's certainly a machine that gives stability and manageability in most road conditions. This is due partly to an engine control unit that can be switched between 'free power' and 'controlled power', for better control of the motorcycle in poor traction conditions. With the 'free power' configuration it's possible to fully experience the torque features and engine power that this exciting machine offers, while the 'controlled power' configuration gives easier and better control in city situations and on asphalt with poor traction. By using the control unit, the added bonus is that you can also achieve better fuel consumption by some 10-20 per cent, depending on how you ride and road conditions.

The TNT Sport offers a great combination of manoeuvrability and brilliant engine performance, along with interesting design details.

SPECIFICATION

Engine:	Four-stroke, three-cylinder, DOHC, 4VPC, in-line, tilted forwards 15°, anti-vibration countershaft
Bore x stroke:	88 x 62 mm
Displacement:	1130cc
Fuel system:	Electronic fuel injection-1 injector per cylinder
Ignition:	Electronic
Cooling system:	Liquid - two radiators, two electronic fans
Gearbox:	Six-speed.
Clutch:	Wet, multi-plate
Primary drive:	Gears
Final drive:	Chain
Frame:	Front ASD steel tube trellis, fastened with drawer screws to boxed rear section - aluminium alloy castings
Front suspension:	Marzocchi 50 mm diameter upside-down fork
Rear suspension:	ASD steel tube trellis oscillating main fork with 'Extreme Technology' monoshock
Brakes	Brembo
Front:	Double floating disk - 320 mm, with radial 4-piston calliper
Rear:	Single disk - 240mm, with twin-piston calliper
Wheels	Die-cast aluminium alloy
Front:	3.5 x 17 in
Rear:	6.0 x 17 in
Tyres	Dunlop Tubeless radial
Front:	D208RR, 120/70 x 17 in
Rear:	D208RR, 190/50 x 17 in
Seat height:	780 mm
Wheelbase:	1419 mm
Dry weight:	199 kg

BIMOTA Tesi
3D Concept

Just one glance at this extreme machine, tells you that it is a further development of the Bimota Tesi series of bikes. As radical as its predecessor and more, this is a stunning looking piece of machinery. This, without doubt, is a bike that will give you large helpings of 'street cred' and with the incredible 1079cc Ducati engine, is without doubt amazingly fast too!

The white, red and gold livery is classic Bimota, and this bike has been designed and built by the fanatical staff at the Rimini factory in Italy. The Tesi 3D Concept is a design that draws on all the engineering skills that Bimota has always been so proud of and dedicated to.

First shown at the EICMA Motorcycle show in Milan in 2006, the Bimota Tesi 3D concept is now a reality. It is everything that Bimota would want it to be, innovative and packed with cutting-edge technology. It oozes Bimota and all that this little company stands for.

The bike still features the original Hub-Steering developed by Bimota, but the Tesi 3D Concept boasts several other new developments and refinements. The front and rear swingarms use a trellis structure, similar to the rear swingarm of their DB5 and DB6 models. The front suspension has been radically redesigned and now uses a pull-rod mechanism, with the hydraulic suspension located low-down beside the engine. Carbon body parts and cowling, forged alloy wheels, and radial disc brakes are further features of the new Tesi 3D.

The Tesi 3D is equipped with a Ducati 1100 DS engine, controlled by a state-of-the-art electronic system developed by Bimota. This exclusive system boosts power output to 95 hp, and torque to 10.5 kg at 5000rpm, while still satisfying the high emission standards imposed by Euro-3.

This is no ordinary machine and for that reason Bimota has decided that only a limited number of examples will be made. Each machine will be identified by a thick gold plate on which the series number and owners name will be placed. Along with this, a bike cover, stand, Bimota jacket and gloves will also be thrown in with the package - a truly unique experience.

SPECIFICATION

Engine:	Ducati L 90° Twin, 2vpc
Bore x stroke:	98 x 71.5mm
Displacement:	1079cc
Fuel System:	Magnetti Marelli injectors. 45mm throttle body, Bitron 3.5 bar, electronic fuel pump.
Ignition:	Electronic.
Exhaust system:	2 into 1 into 2.
Lubrication:	Wet sump.
Gearbox:	Six-speed.
Clutch:	Oil bath, multi-disc, Hydraulic Device Control.
Primary drive:	Gear.
Final drive:	Chain.
Frame:	Omega machined aluminium alloy.
Suspension	
Front:	Monoshock Pull-Rod Extreme Tech, fully adjustable.
Rear:	Monoshock Extreme Tech, fully adjustable.
Brakes	Brembo
Front:	320 mm twin, floating discs. Radial callipers, four-piston, four pads.
Rear:	220 mm disc. Two-pistons, two pads.
Wheels	Forged aluminium alloy
Front:	3.50 x 17 in
Rear:	5.50 x 17 in
Tyres	Dunlop D208RR
Front:	120/70 ZR 17
Rear:	180/55 ZR 17
Overall length:	2000 mm
Overall width:	720 mm
Overall height:	1140 mm
Seat height:	800 mm
Wheelbase:	1390 mm
Dry weight:	168 kg
Tank capacity:	16 litres

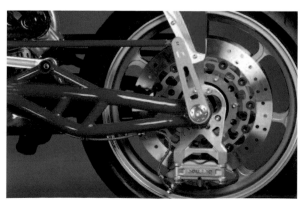

While the 3D still features the original hub-steering developed by Bimota, there are several new developments and refinements. The front and rear swing utilise a trellis structure, as seen here.

The Ducati 1100 DS engine, which has a displacement of 1079cc and is controlled by a state-of-the-art electronic system developed by Bimota, is seen here enveloped by its housing.

BMW K1200 S

Several years ago, BMW made a decision to enter the sports segment of the motorcycle market and create a machine that would serve as a prestigious and exciting top-end addition to their current model line-up. The aim was for this motorcycle to attain the same level of desirability and reputation that has always been enjoyed by BMW's M-division performance cars.

It was never BMW Motorrad's intention to create a super-sports motorcycle designed and engineered for the racetrack rather than the road, or to produce a hyper-sport machine with the highest possible top speed. BMW Motorrad's intention was to design a machine that would complement and straddle both categories, and which would also attract customers from the high-performance sports touring sector of the market.

With the launch of the new K1200 S, BMW introduced a motorcycle that was lighter and more agile than a hyper-sports machine, but just as fast, as dynamic on the track as a super-sports machine, but far more usable in everyday riding situations.

Superiority in suspension design, with electronic adjustability options, firmly establishes the K1200 S as the most technologically advanced motorcycle available.

This was a machine that would attempt to attract those riders who were tired of machines that only performed in a straight line, or only performed at their best on a race circuit. This machine would show them that it was possible to have immense but usable horsepower, significant high-speed capability, and unquestionable ergonomic efficiency without compromising BMW's legendary comfort levels, fuel efficiency and distance capability.

ENGINE

Fitted crosswise, the straight-four power unit of the BMW K1200 S displaces 1157cc. Maximum output is 123 kW (167 bhp) at 10,250 rpm; maximum torque of 130 Nm (96 lb-ft) is delivered at 8,250 rpm - with more than 70 per cent of the engine's maximum torque available from just 3,000 rpm. The engine power is easy to control at all times, which was BMW Motorrad's clear-cut objective when developing the new machine. Weighing just 81.3 kg (179.3 lb) including the clutch and gearbox, the engine is one of the lightest of its size in the market.

SPECIFICATION

Engine:	In-line, four-cylinder, DOHC, 4VPC
Bore x stroke:	79 x 59 mm
Displacement:	1157cc
Fuel system:	BMSK
Ignition:	Electric starter
Gearbox:	Six-speed, claw-shifted
Clutch:	Multi-plate oil bath clutch. 151 mm diameter
Primary drive:	Chain
Final drive:	Driveshaft
Frame:	Composite aluminium with IHU/extrusion-pressed profiles and die sections
Front suspension:	BMW Duolever
Rear suspension:	BMW Paralever
Brakes	BMW Motorrad integral ABS fitted as standard
Front:	Double disc - 320 mm
Rear:	Single disc - 265 mm
Wheels:	Light alloy
Front:	3.50 x 17 MTH 2
Rear:	6.00 x 17 MTH 2
Tyres	
Front:	120/70 XR 17
Rear:	190/50 ZR 17
Overall length:	2282 mm
Overall width:	905 mm with mirrors
Seat height:	820 mm
Wheelbase:	1571 mm
Weight:	248 kg - unladen, with full tank
Tank capacity:	19 litres

The wing mirrors of the K1200 S also house the front indicators - practical and neat design feature.

A comprehensive array of instruments - tachometer, speedometer and a digital display, keep the rider extremely well informed.

The K 1200 S complies fully with environmental requirements, thanks to highly advanced emission management and a fully controlled three-way catalytic converter

BMW R1200 S

When the BMW R1100 S was launched in 1998 it was the most powerful Boxer in the history of BMW Motorrad, with 98 hp and 97 Nm of torque. The air-cooled horizontal twin inspired the popular and spectacular International Boxer Cup race series and became the BMW of choice for many motorcyclists who appreciated its true sporting capabilities, despite the fact that it was built uncompromisingly for the road. It remained largely unchanged throughout its eight-year life cycle and, unlike all the other models in BMW's Boxer line-up, never appeared in an 1150cc engine configuration.

Proudly making its debut in 2006 and aimed primarily at the pure sports end of the market was the new R1200 S - the most powerful production Boxer the world has ever seen.

This new sports Boxer shares little with its predecessor and neatly fills the gap between BMW Motorrad's four-cylinder K1200 S and single-cylinder F800 S sports bikes.

With this new sports bike, BMW were looking to tempt riders away from Japanese and Italian 'supersport' machines that were too closely modelled on factory race bikes, to actually be practical in everyday riding conditions. They are sure that despite the R1200 S's undoubted track capabilities an overwhelming number of owners will only ever ride the S on the road.

ENGINE

BMW's new sports Boxer displaces 1170cc, with the two-cylinders featuring four valves and two spark plugs per cylinder. The modified cylinder heads enable the R1200 S to develop an impressive 90 kW/122 hp, smoothly delivered to the crankshaft running in anti-friction bearings. Power is transmitted via new, high load-resistant connecting rods, made of extra-strong steel alloy. Harder valve springs and reinforced rocker arms take the high speed of the engine of up to 8,800 rpm into account, a speed level incidentally never seen before on a BMW Boxer.

Tucked away here is the highly flexible, maintenance-free shaft drive along with the single-sided swinging arm.

SPECIFICATION

Engine:	Flat twin, 4VPC
Bore x stroke:	101 x 73 mm
Displacement:	1170cc
Fuel system:	BMS-K
Ignition:	Electric starter
Gearbox:	Six-speed, dog-shifted
Clutch:	Single-plate, dry clutch
Primary drive:	Chain
Final drive:	Driveshaft
Frame:	Main and front frame - steel tubes; rear frame - square aluminium tubes
Front suspension:	BMW Telelever
Rear suspension:	BMW Paralever
Brakes:	BMW Motorrad integral ABS fitted as standard
Front:	Double disc - 320 mm
Rear:	Single disc - 265 mm
Wheels:	Light alloy
Front:	3.50 x 17 in
Rear:	5.50 x 17 in
Tyres	
Front:	120/70 ZR 17
Rear:	180/55 ZR 17
Overall length:	2151 mm
Overall width:	870 mm with mirrors
Seat height:	830 mm
Wheelbase:	1571 mm
Weight:	213 kg in road trim
Tank capacity:	17 litres

Easy to read instrumentation - a mix of analogue and digital displays - helps the rider to keep an eye on what is going on.

A neat styling touch, the silencer with tailpipes are positioned beneath one another directly under the rear fairing.

BUELL
Lightning Super TT XB12STT

The Super TT is a further addition to the Lightning family. By taking elements from the others in the range this machine is ideally suited to tackle the tough and dangerous roads of any city, as well as being able to get your adrenalin pumping on the long twisty black-tops of the countryside. Although it has a clearly aggressive look, it isn't too wild to tame. Acceleration is not its strong point, but take it out on the long winding roads and suddenly you know why Buell made this bike. The handling is magic and once you start to hang that knee out you won't want to stop - sheer delight urging you onto the next corner.

The main emphasis of this machine, like most Buell bikes, is to concentrate all the mass weight at the centre of the bike - right underneath the rider. Also, by keeping as much weight in the centre of the machine and as low as possible, it will give a much better centre of gravity and thus a better handling bike. Better distribution of braking forces is also attained by positioning the disc brake on the rim of the front wheel, rather than at the centre.

The Super TT is the latest addition to the Buell Lightning family. By combining two areas of motorcycling styles it classes itself as part road racer, part dirt tracker and part motocrosser. Stubby looks and low centre of gravity give it charisma and stability, all realised through the Buell philosophy.

The powerful Thunderstorm 1203cc 45° engine responds well in confined city spaces and loves to be opened up once out on the open road. The engine has been tuned for the rider who is happy to have a smooth and torquey throttle response rather than a sudden rush of speed, although it has to be said this machine is no slouch! Much technical thought has been given to the exhaust and engine management system, to give the best possible performance whilst also keeping in mind the restrictive European noise and emission regulations.

Buell machines have always been innovative in their design and the TT is no different. The lightweight aluminium frame contains the fuel and the swingarm doubles up as the oil reservoir. As with the other models in the Lightning family the silencer is located below the engine and final drive is via a durable Goodyear Hibrex final drive belt with Flexten Plus technology, and requires no scheduled service or replacement.

The Super TT has a competition-inspired look, including racing-style number plates, white Surlyn flyscreen and a small satin black tail piece. These are just a few of the parts that can make your machine personal to you, as they are just asking to be customised.

The small but efficient front flyscreen sits above the twin lights, which are protected by two bars.

The instrument panel is neatly tucked away from harm behind the flyscreen.

The lightweight aluminium frame acts as the fuel reservoir, the swingarm holds the engine oil and the silencer is located directly below the engine.

The TT is a great-looking machine, enhanced by its side number plates and front mini flyscreen. Leave it somewhere too long and it will attract a crowd of inquisitive onlookers. Starting is simple, there is no choke, and when you accelerate away the engine gives out a lovely kind of 'puffy throb' as it gets into its stride with determination. The machine sits high at the saddle and is only suitable for one person - no footpegs, no passengers!

SPECIFICATION

Engine:	Four-stroke, OHV, 2VPC, 45° V-Twin
Bore x stroke:	88.9 x 96.8 mm
Displacement:	1203cc
Fuel system:	Down-draft DDFI II fuel injection - 49 mm
Ignition:	Electric starter
Exhaust:	Tuned, tri-pass resonance chamber with InterActive valve and mass-centralised mounting
Lubrication:	Dry sump
Gearbox:	Five-speed, helical gears
Clutch:	Wet, multi-plate
Primary drive:	Chain
Final drive:	Constant path, 14mm aramid-reinforced Hibrex belt, with Flexten Plus technology
Frame:	Aluminium with Uniplaner powertrain vibration isolation system - fuel in frame
Front suspension:	Showa 43 mm inverted forks
Rear suspension:	Showa coil-over monoshock
Brakes	
Front:	ZTL type brake, six-piston, fixed calliper, 375 mm single-sided, inside-out, stainless steel floating rotor
Rear:	Single-piston, floating calliper, 240 mm stainless steel fixed rotor
Wheels:	Cast aluminium
Front:	6-spoke, ZTL, 3.5 x 17 in
Rear:	6-spoke, 5.5 x 17 in
	Tyres Pirelli - Scorpion Sync
Front:	120/70 ZR 17
Rear:	180/55 ZR 17
Overall length:	2,080 mm
Overall width:	820 mm
Seat height:	798 mm standard
Wheelbase:	1,365 mm
Dry weight:	179 kg
Tank capacity:	16.7 litres

Dodge Tomahawk

The Tomahawk was a concept that left the people attending the 2003 Detroit Auto Show, open mouthed. Better known for their cars and trucks, Dodge introduced this potentially capable 400 mph-plus concept motorcycle, and dared people to believe it!

Just nine months after its sensational unveiling at the 2003 Detroit Auto Show, DaimlerChrysler announced that this mega-machine would become a very exclusive and limited production motorcycle. There would be an initial replica model and possibly a further nine to follow. As a concept it was never really meant to go into general production, although the up-market catalogue company from Dallas, Neiman Marcus, did include it in their Christmas 2003 booklet - each example would have a price tag of US$555,000.

The Tomahawk's monocoque chassis and billet aluminium frame, hold the 8300cc/505 cu in, V-10 Dodge Viper engine, which is capable of producing a hefty 525 lb/ft of rear-wheel torque. The motorcycle has the unique characteristic of having two wheels closely positioned at the front and at the rear, and has a dual centre hub steering mechanism, for what is reportedly impressive traction. The running prototype estimated a 0-60 mph time of just 2.5 seconds and a calculated top speed in excess of 310 mph.

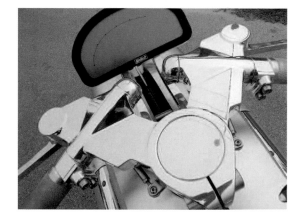

The Tomahawk uses dual hub center type steering. Steering lock is 20 degrees, left and right, the lean angle is 45 degrees, left and right.

This is the 10-cylinder, 90-degree, V-type, liquid-cooled, 8275cc engine, which has an aluminium alloy block with cast-iron liners and aluminium alloy cylinder heads.

Dodge Tomahawk Concept Preliminary Specifications:

Engine:	505 cu in/8300cc aluminium Viper V-10 engine
Suspension:	Four-wheel independent suspension
Horsepower/torque:	500 hp/525 lb/ft of torque
Estimated top speed:	Potentially 420 mph

DUCATI 1098 S and Tricolore

A celebration of Italian culture.

The introduction of the Ducati 1098 was a welcome return to the classic Ducati shape and style. There is no doubting the greatness of the previous models but this new 1098 had styling that aligned itself to the earlier 916, a machine that even today will make anybody's head turn. The 916 has become a legend and there is little doubt that the 1098 will go the same way.

A tradition that was started back in 1985 with the 750 F1, and then continued with the limited edition 851, has been extended to the 1098 for 2007. Ducati have released the special edition 1098 S Tricolore (triple colour), which sees this amazing-looking machine decorated in the vibrant colours of the Italian national flag - red, white and green.

There is little to differentiate the Tricolore from the original bike except of course the colour scheme. It too comes supplied with the Ducati Data Analyzer (DDA) system as standard equipment. The DDA package supplied with the 'S' version enables the retrieval of data, and the analysis of data collected from a previous track session or road trip. The DDA package includes software for personal computer on CD, data retrieval USB key and instructions. As if the bike wasn't powerful enough already, a power-increasing 102 dB Termignoni racing muffler kit with dedicated ECU, is also supplied with the bike.

Just in case you don't hear this beautiful machine approaching, additional features include the frame and wheels being finished in traditional 'racing gold' colours. It will stand out amongst the rest!

ENGINE

The Testastretta Evoluzione engine is the crowning glory of Ducati's development and perfection of the L-Twin engine. World Superbike dominance for the last fifteen years is the result of continual commitment to twin-cylinder technology and the 1098 Testastretta Evoluzione, the most powerful twin-cylinder production engine in history, is a fitting reward to the Ducati engineers' continued ingenuity. The 1098 engine is immediately recognisable by its completely new compact cylinders and cylinder heads. Other 1098 innovations and revisions are less obvious as they reside within the Evoluzione's engine cases. Many small but significant changes and adjustments have been made to this new Testastretta engine, so that even the standard specification 1098 produces more power than the previous extreme Testastretta 'R' engine. The Testastretta Evoluzione is also the lightest Ducati Superbike engine ever produced.

The lightweight 2-1-2 exhaust system culminates in under-seat twin stainless steel silencers.

The fully adjustable Öhlins 46PRC rear shock with ride enhancing top-out spring, controlling the single-sided swingarm.

Digital MotoGP derived unit displaying all the usual information plus average speed, average fuel consumption and remaining fuel metre.

Final drive is via a sealed chain and sprocket, the rear wheel is by Marchesini. The hole in the middle is for a single-sided racing stand.

At the front end of this beautiful machine are twin headlights, encased in a superbly aerodynamic fairing.

SPECIFICATION

Engine:	L-Twin cylinder, 4VPC, Desmodromic, liquid cooled.
Bore x stroke:	104 x 64.7 mm
Displacement:	1099cc
Fuel system:	Marelli electronic fuel injection, elliptical throttle bodies
Exhaust:	Lightweight, 2-1-2 system with catalytic converter and lambda probe. Twin stainless with a 102 dB Termignoni racing muffler kit in carbon fibre complete with dedicated ECU Emissions Euro3
Gearbox:	Six-speed
Clutch:	Dry multi-plate with hydraulic control
Primary drive:	Straight-cut gears
Final drive:	Chain
Frame:	Tubular steel trellis in ALS 450
Front suspension:	Öhlins 43 mm fully adjustable upside-down fork with TiN
Rear suspension:	Progressive linkage with fully adjustable Öhlins monoshock with top-out spring. Aluminium single-sided swingarm
Brakes	
Front:	2 x 330 mm semi-floating discs, radially mounted Brembo Monobloc callipers, 4-piston, 2-pad
Rear:	245 mm disc, 2-piston calliper
Wheels:	5-spoke Marchesini in forged and machined light alloy
Front:	3.50 x 17 in
Rear:	6.00 x 17 in
Tyres	
Front:	120/70 ZR 17
Rear:	190/55 ZR 17
Seat height:	820 mm / 32.2 in
Wheelbase:	1430 mm / 56.3 in
Weight:	171 kg / 377 lb (excludes battery, lubricants and, where applicable, cooling liquid)
Tank capacity:	15.5 litres, 4 litre reserve

DUCATI
Desmosedici RR

Ducati launched the Desmosedici RR production prototype during the magical atmosphere of the 2006 Italian Grand Prix at Mugello. For those riders who were desperately hoping, the dream of a real GP replica had finally come true. The stunning Desmosedici RR will be the first ever road-going motorcycle to offer the incredible performance and technology taken directly from MotoGP. The RR is derived from the Ducati Corse Grand Prix racing Desmosedici GP6 machine, the same bike which Loris Capirossi and Sete Gibernau used to compete in the 2006 MotoGP World Championship.

The aerodynamic body is designed faithfully to reflect the Desmosedici GP6. The colour scheme, components and materials used in its construction, as well as the technical features of the powerful four-cylinder Desmodromic engine, built by the Borgo Panigale factory engineers, leaves no doubts whatsoever - the Desmosedici RR is the ultimate road expression of the most extreme MotoGP racing machine today.

Capirossi seen during the 2006 MotoGP season. This is the machine that inspired Ducati to introduce their replica road-going version. An ensemble of sheer beauty and poetic motion that few others could possibly dream of creating.

The Ducati Desmosedici RR features the most advanced technology and aerodynamics derived directly from the GP6 raced in the 2006 MotoGP World Championship. The engine of the Desmosedici RR accurately reflects that of the MotoGP bike. Ducati's traditional Desmodromic system guarantees precise valve control at the very highest revs and is the perfect application for the 989cc, four titanium valves per cylinder, L-Four layout.
This awesome powerplant, which is prepared in asymmetrical Twin Pulse configuration, is a masterwork of precision engineering.

The double overhead cams are gear-driven, a sophisticated and reliable solution that enables precise valve timing in all conditions. This authentic copy of the GP engine is further endorsed by the use of a cassette-type six-speed gearbox and hydraulically actuated dry multi-plate slipper clutch.

The smooth lines of the RR are down to the aerodynamics package which is aimed at achieving maximum speed and excellent handling.

SPECIFICATION

Engine:	Desmodromic system, 4VPC, L-Four, DOHC
Displacement:	989cc
Fuel system:	Four 50 mm Magneti Marelli throttle bodies and 12-hole 'microjet' injectors
Ignition:	A Magneti Marelli 5SM ECU and high-speed CAN line electronics
Exhaust:	4-2-1 system, with 'vertical exit' silencer
Gearbox:	Six-speed, cassette type
Clutch:	Dry multi-plate slipper type
Primary drive:	Gear driven
Final drive:	Chain
Frame:	Tubular steel trellis hybrid frame (ALS 450); rear subframe in high-temperature resin-type carbon fibre.New extra-long, cast, forged and pressed aluminium alloy swingarm
Front suspension:	Öhlins 'FG353' PFF forks USD 43 mm pressurised, with preload, rebound and compression adjustment, TiN coated sliders
Rear suspension:	Öhlins rear shock, with rebound, low/high speed compression adjustment, and hydraulic preload adjustment
Brakes	Brembo
Front:	Two Brembo radial Monobloc callipers with four 34 mm pistons; two semi-floating 320 mm x 6 mm discs, with machined flange: the same as GP6 wet race set-up
Rear:	240 mm fixed disc, calliper with two 34 mm pistons
Wheels:	Marchesini forged and machined magnesium alloy, 7-spoke design as GP6.
Tyres:	Bridgestone
Available with:	Special race kit including 102dB racing exhaust, dedicated CPU, bike cover and paddock stand
Versions: 1.	The 'Desmosedici RR' finished in 'Rosso GP' with white number plate on the tail-section
Versions: 2.	The 'Desmosedici RR Team Version' finished in 'Rosso GP' with broad white stripe on the fairing as per Factory race bikes

The colour scheme of the Desmosedici RR was the work of Alan Jenkins, the designer and one of the men behind the Desmosedici MotoGP machine.

The bike's development could not have been made possible without the significant collaboration of Vittoriano Guareschi, the official Ducati Corse test rider.

Ducati Monster S4R S Testastretta

Designed for the most experienced riders who expect the very best in terms of technology, performance and componentry, the Monster S4R S Testastretta benefits from the Ducati experience gained in the World Superbike Championship. The liquid-cooled, four-valve per cylinder, 998 Testastretta L-Twin engine features a 100 mm bore and short stroke of 63.5 mm to limit average piston speed and allow increased rpm. The result is a staggering 130 hp and 10.6 kg of brute torque.

Fully adjustable Öhlins suspension front and rear complemented by lightweight Y-shaped five-spoke wheels ensure outstanding handling, while 320 mm Brembo twin discs on the front have radial-mounted callipers with four pistons and pads per calliper to provide rigidly mounted, powerful brakes with incredible stopping power. And to make this Monster look even more exciting and contribute to its overall light weight is the use of carbon fibre for the silencer cover, exhaust heat plate, front mudguard, radiator covers and cam belt covers.

SPECIFICATION

Engine:	L-twin cylinder, 4VPC, Testastretta Desmodromic, liquid cooled	**Brakes**		
		Front:	2 x 320 mm discs, 4-piston 4-pad radial calliper	
Bore x stroke:	100 x 63.5 mm	**Rear:**	245 mm disc, 2-piston calliper	
Displacement:	998cc	**Wheels**	5-spoke light alloy	
Fuel system:	Marelli electronic fuel injection, 50 mm throttle body	**Front:**	3.50 x 17 in	
		Rear:	5.50 x 17 in	
Exhaust:	Two aluminium silencers	**Tyres**		
Gearbox:	Six-speed	**Front:**	120/70 ZR 17	
Clutch:	Dry multi-plate with hydraulic control	**Rear:**	180/55 ZR 17	
Primary drive:	Straight-cut gears	**Seat height:**	800 mm	
Final drive:	Chain	**Wheelbase:**	1440 mm	
Frame:	Tubular steel trellis	**Overall weight:**	177 kg (excludes battery, lubricants and cooling liquid).	
Front suspension:	Öhlins 43 mm upside-down fully adjustable fork with TiN	**Tank capacity:**	14 litres (3 litre reserve)	
Rear suspension:	Progressive linkage with fully adjustable Öhlins monoshock. Aluminium single-sided swingarm			

The right side of the bike is dominated by the twin silencer units that tuck neatly into the rear of the machine.

Seen from the rear the Monster has pleasing bodywork features that integrate well with the standard Ducati trellis framework.

Honda
CBR1000RR
Fireblade

The original Fireblade was launched back in 1992 and took the motorcycling world by storm. It had all the ingredients of a great machine and its aggressive Super Sports-styled bodywork, highlighted by the tiger-stripe pattern paint job, set it apart from all the other bikes of the period.

It was a stunningly good-looking machine right from day one, and as the years have passed the Fireblade has lost none of its class and charm. It has not only kept up with, but also inspired new design and stunning looks. The Fireblade is still a truly desirable machine, not only for track work but for day-to-day use too.

Besides its good looks the 'Blade', as it is often fondly referred to, has also become more powerful over the years. From the original 893cc engine it has progressed to the latest compact, mass-centralised, in-line, four-cylinder 998cc power unit, force-fed by the latest Honda fuel injection system, helping to generate that all so awesome power.

Just having a good-looking machine is not enough to make it as stunningly fast and manageable as it is though. The hollow-section, die-cast aluminium frame, inverted front fork and swingarm-integrated Unit Pro-Link rear suspension, all contribute to give the precise handling that this handsome machine delivers. A unique and highly innovative electronic steering damper also helps to keep you in control when strafing those corners on the ragged edge of performance. So whether you are just going out for a Sunday ride to meet friends, or ready to put in a stunning lap on the race circuit, the 'Blade' is capable of coping with both situations, giving you inspiration and confidence.

To celebrate Honda's long, fruitful and continuing association with Spanish oil company Repsol YPF on the Motorcycle Grand Prix and MotoGP circuits, Honda has proudly announced the release of a special version of its best-selling CBR1000RR Fireblade. Having captured the 2006 Constructors' and Teams' Championships at the Japan round of the Grand Prix series, the team went on to see Nicky Hayden capture the Riders' Championship at the controls of his powerful RC211V racer.

There isn't too much one can say that hasn't already been said about the Fireblade. It is a well matured piece of machinery that gives its rider heaps of pleasure. It always creates interest wherever it goes and has become a legend in its own lifetime. For 2007, Honda introduce a celebratory machine (above) decked out in the racing colour scheme used by Nicky Hayden and his MotoGP team, after their championship winning season of 2006.

SPECIFICATION

Engine:	Liquid-cooled, four-stroke, 16-valve, DOHC, in-line, four-cylinders
Bore x stroke:	75 x 56.5 mm
Displacement:	998cc
Fuel system:	Carburation PGM-DSFI electronic fuel injection throttle bore 44 mm
Ignition system:	Computer-controlled digital transistorised with electronic advance
Exhaust:	4 into 2 into 1 with EGCV valve and catalytic converter
Lubrication:	Wet sump
Gearbox:	Six-speed
Clutch:	Wet, multi-plate with coil springs. Hydraulic operation
Primary drive:	Straight-cut gears with bearing selection for optimum mesh
Final drive:	Sealed chain
Frame:	Diamond, aluminium composite twin-spar
Front suspension:	43mm inverted HMAS cartridge-type telescopic fork
Rear suspension:	Unit Pro-Link with gas-charged HMAS damper
Brakes	
Front:	320 x 4.5 mm dual hydraulic disc with 4-piston callipers and sintered metal pads
Rear:	220 x 5 mm hydraulic disc with single-piston calliper and sintered metal pads
Wheels:	Hollow-section triple-spoke cast aluminium
Front:	17M/C x MT3.5
Rear:	17M/C x MT6
Tyres	
Front:	120/70-ZR17M/C (58W)
Rear:	190/50-ZR17M/C (73W)
Overall length:	2,030 mm
Overall width:	720 mm
Overall height:	1,118 mm
Seat height:	831 mm
Wheelbase:	1,400 mm
Dry weight:	176 kg
Tank capacity:	18 litres (4 litre reserve)

The gas-charged HMAS damper featuring 13-step preload and stepless compression and rebound damping adjustment.

Large and very clear instrumentation with warning lights neatly placed at either side of the tacho.

Aerodynamically honed to give the best airflow possible, the front of the fairing incorporates twin headlights.

The twin silencers are neatly tucked away under the rear seat panel, protruding like twin barrels of a shot-gun.

Honda VTR1000 SP-2

It was during 2000 that Honda launched its original VTR1000 SP-1. A totally new 1000cc, V-twin machine based on VTR1000F, but with stronger power and reliability for consistent racing class levels of performance. Along with its lightweight HRC developed wheels, designed to easily mount racing slicks, there was also an optional HRC-produced racing kit. Ridden in the World Superbike races during 2001 by Colin Edwards, Honda picked up the championship this same year.

Just two years later in 2002 the VTR1000 SP-2 made its debut, with the engine modified for stronger and smoother performance, a stronger and lighter new HRC-based press-forged aluminium swingarm, lighter front fork and more easily adjustable Works-type rear damper, along with new five-spoke wheels. Once again ridden by Edwards, Honda picked up the World Superbike championship this year too.

The VTR1000 SP-2 is essentially a street-legal racing machine equipped with many of the technological advances seen on Honda's earlier Superbike championship machine. This machine doesn't wait for you to ask, it just goes and delivers a breathtaking rush of acceleration from pretty well anywhere in its broad powerband. Although very capable on the track, the SP-2 is also remarkably agile and well-sorted for use on the normal road.

The SP-2 lost its position in Superbike racing when the rules were changed to encourage more official team participation. With the rule changes the four-cylinder machines, in particular the CBR1000RR Fireblade, became the machines to race because of the added power and general specification.

SPECIFICATION

Engine:	Liquid-cooled, four-stroke, eight-valve, DOHC, 90° V-twin	**Rear:**	Pro-Link with gas-charged integrated remote reservoir damper
Bore x stroke:	100 x 63.6 mm	**Brakes**	
Displacement:	999cc	**Front:**	320 x 5 mm dual hydraulic disc with 4-piston callipers, floating rotors and sintered metal pads
Fuel system:	PGM-FI electronic fuel injection. Throttle bore 62 mm		
Ignition:	Computer-controlled digital transistorised with electronic advance	**Rear:**	220 x 5 mm hydraulic disc with single-piston calliper and sintered metal pads
Exhaust:	2 into 1 into 2	**Wheels**	V-section, 5-spoke cast aluminium
Lubrication:	Wet sump	**Front:**	17M/C x MT3.5
Gearbox:	Six-speed	**Rear:**	17M/C x MT6
Clutch:	Wet, multi-plate with coil springs. Hydraulic operation	**Tyres**	
		Front:	120/70-ZR17M/C (58W)
Primary drive:	Straight-cut gears with anti-backlash	**Rear:**	190/50-ZR17M/C (73W)
Final drive:	Sealed chain	**Overall length:**	2,040 mm
Frame:	Diamond, triple-box-section aluminium twin-spar	**Overall width:**	725 mm
		Overall height:	1,145 mm
Suspension		**Seat height:**	825 mm
Front:	43 mm inverted cartridge-type fork with adjustable spring preload	**Wheelbase:**	1,420 mm
		Dry weight:	194 kg
		Fuel tank capacity:	18 litres (2.5 litre warning light reserve)

Honda CBR1100XX Super Blackbird

The Blackbird most people think about is a larger-than-life bird, that steals all the bread thrown out for the little red breasted Robin….oooh! On the other hand if you were aviation-inclined, you would probably relate to the spy plane that travels at a staggering speed of Mach 3, and which held the record for the quickest trans-Atlantic flight….wow!

Well the Blackbird that we are featuring here is neither of those, but you could say that it does retain some characteristics from both these flying objects - it's very aerodynamic, it's built for speed and it was once the fastest production bike in the world, and so it was only right that it should take its name from the supersonic aircraft of the same name. In fact it is the extraordinarily beautiful CBR1100XX Super Blackbird motorcycle. This is a machine that could be classed as a perfect outcome for what it was designed - high speed touring.

Keeping in mind that the Blackbird is a touring machine, having good, clear instrumentation is essential.

Essential grab-handle for the passenger also incorporates toggles, which can be used for attaching bungee-straps and the like.

Although the first CBR1100XX Super Blackbird made its debut in 1997 as Honda's new high-speed Super Sports flagship, some essential changes have taken place - fuel injection, better performance brakes and suspension improvements, just to name a few.

This Blackbird was made for long-distance touring and it does that with ease. Just get on one of these machines and run it down the road and you will feel the potential power, the comfort of the seat and the well sculpted and aerodynamically efficient fairing. The big 1100cc engine purrs with delight, turning into an awesome tarmac-eating machine as soon as you twist the accelerator grip. Everything about this bike is calculated and easy to use; the engine delivers power as smooth as you like, and when you finally decide you want to slow or stop, the dual combined brakes jump into action with precision from any speed. If touring is your game, then there can be no better recommendation than the Super Blackbird it meets all the criteria and performs well on long straight motorways as well as being steady and stable on the twisty bits too.

SPECIFICATION

Engine:	Liquid-cooled, four-stroke, 16-valve, DOHC, in-line, four-cylinders
Bore x stroke:	79 x 58 mm
Displacement:	1,137cc
Fuel system:	PGM-FI electronic fuel injection. 42 mm throttle bore
Ignition:	Computer-controlled digital transistorised with electronic advance
Exhaust:	4 into 2 into 1 into 2 with catalytic converter
Lubrication:	Wet sump
Gearbox:	Six-speed
Clutch:	Wet, multi-plate with coil springs. Hydraulic operation
Primary drive:	Straight-cut gears with anti-backlash
Final drive:	Sealed chain
Frame:	Diamond, triple-box-section aluminium twin-spar
Suspension	
Front:	43 mm H.M.A.S. cartridge-type telescopic fork
Rear:	Pro-Link with gas-charged H.M.A.S. damper
Brakes	
Front:	310 x 5 mm dual hydraulic disc with combined 3-piston callipers and sintered metal pads
Rear:	256 x 5 mm hydraulic disc with combined 3-piston calliper and sintered metal pads
Wheels	Hollow-section triple-spoke cast aluminium
Front:	17 x MT3.5
Rear:	17 x MT5.5
Tyres	
Front:	120/70-ZR17 (58W)
Rear:	180/55-ZR17 (73W)
Overall length:	2,160 mm
Overall width:	720 mm
Overall height:	1,200 mm
Seat Height:	810 mm
Wheelbase:	1,490 mm
Dry weight:	227 kg
Tank capacity:	23 litres (4 litre warning light reserve)

The mirrors also have a double function and incorporate the left and right front indicators.

The fairing of the Blackbird has had many hours of aerodynamic testing carried out on it, so that the rider and passenger can ride at speed, in comfort.

Kawasaki ZZR1400

It's well over a year since the Kawasaki Ninja ZZR1400 made its debut in March of 2006, and it has won every major magazine comparison test it has participated in, earning universal praise for massive torque, effortless power, stable handling and a comfortable riding position: the 1352cc Ninja ZZR1400 has set the highest performance standard in the motorcycle industry.

It's never easy to use the word 'ultimate' when talking about motorcycles, as once you do, you tend to get caught out! Just taking a look back at legendary machines such as the Z1 and GPZ900R, to modern hyper-bikes like the ZZ-R1100, Kawasaki's flagship machines have set the pace for others to followed. The incredible ZZR1400 is a machine which delivers levels of performance and excitement that is hard to beat, and continues that tradition of leadership.

The new ZZR1400 is powered by an all-new engine, force-fed with Ram Air and fuel injection. This machine churns out unheard-of levels of thrust and yet in spite of the incredible performance of Kawasaki's most powerful power plant ever, careful engine tuning allows almost anyone to enjoy the bike's softer, more rider-friendly side. The power that this machine develops has to be matched with its handling characteristics too, and this is taken in hand by Kawasaki's next generation aluminium monocoque frame, that gives the bike both responsive handling qualities and incredible highway stability.

A machine with the power of the ZZR1400 needs incredibly good stopping power. Four-piston, four-pad callipers and vented discs see to that.

SPECIFICATION

Engine type:	Four-stroke, liquid-cooled, DOHC, 4VPC, four-cylinder
Bore x stroke:	84.0 x 61.0 mm
Displacement:	1352cc
Fuel system:	DFI with Mikuni 44 mm throttle bodies (4)
Ignition:	TCBI with Digital Advance
Exhaust:	4 - 1 - 2.
Lubrication:	Forced, wet sump
Gearbox:	Six-speed
Clutch:	Wet, multi-disc
Primary drive:	Gear.
Final Drive:	Chain
Frame:	Monocoque, aluminium
Suspension	
Front:	43 mm inverted cartridge fork, with adjustable preload. 11-way rebound damping, 13-way compression damping with top out springs
Rear:	Bottom-Link Uni-Trak, with gas-charged shock, adjustable preload and stepless rebound/compression damping
Brakes	
Front:	Dual semi-floating 310 mm petal discs, dual radial-mount, opposed four-piston, four-pad calliper
Rear:	Single 250 mm petal disc. Opposed two-piston calliper
Wheels	
Front:	17 in
Rear:	17 in
Tyres	
Front:	120/70ZR17M/C
Rear:	190/50ZR17M/C
Overall length:	85.4 in
Overall width:	29.9 in
Overall height:	46.1 in
Seat height:	31.5 in
Wheelbase:	57.5 in
Dry weight:	474 lb
Tank capacity:	5.8 gal

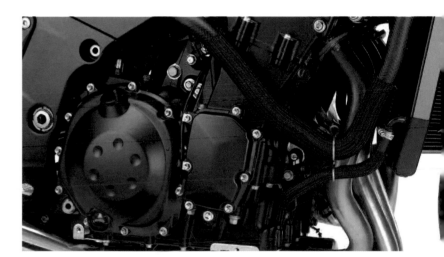

The heart of the machine, an all-new engine, force-fed with Ram Air and fuel injection. The ZZR1400 churns out unheard of levels of thrust, with the greatest of ease.

Nestled in the canopy is an instrument cluster with dual analogue speedometer and tachometer, along with multi-function LCD digital display. White faces make them easy to read.

Kawasaki ZX10R Ninja

I was reading an article on the ZX10R on a website the other day, at the end of which comments were invited. One particular comment caught my eye: 'How do you get rid of the chip that limits the bike to 186?' I have to admit this brought a broad smile to my face.

Kawasaki is no stranger to the land of 'the fastest production bike on earth' title; they have collected that accolade several times and they seem to pride themselves on producing some pretty hair-raisingly fast machines, which of course they do. Having collected the Best Superbike award from Cycle World in both 2004 and 2005, you would imagine that Kawasaki would be happy to leave the breathtaking ZX10 as it was, but NO! The latest model has been updated and uprated, and will enhance the riding pleasure of both road-riders and track racers alike. The awesome just got…er…more awesome?!

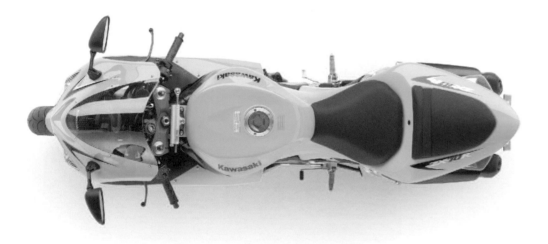

The ZX-10R was designed to be ridden on the circuit, although it is also quite happy on the highway too. The chassis has been reconfigured to reduce lap times, the engine output remains phenomenal and the aerodynamic performance has also been improved. This is a serious track-oriented bike, developed for supersport riders looking for high excitement in the one litre-class. Riders seriously considering competition will find the 10R to be an excellent racing platform.

If you thought that the ZX10R was the ultimate, well wait and see what the men in white jackets at Kawasaki have done with this already stunning machine. Whether you just like to ride fast on the road or you want to take that ride of a lifetime on the track, this machine will astound you. It was already good but now it's even better. Both aerodynamics and chassis configuration have been altered for better performance, even more power has been unleashed from the engine, the chassis has been given revised geometry to centralise the mass, and the swingarm pivot has been relocated in the hunt for better traction from the rear. Although the suspension units and other overall modifications have taken place, these will only be noticed when you check your lap times. For those dedicated track animals, the 10R now also has a race-quality steering damper fitted as standard. Enjoy!

For 2007 the 10R received an all-new aerodynamics package that made it even more slippery through the air. The chassis runs with revised geometry, more centralised mass, a relocated swingarm pivot, revised stiffness balance, re-tuned suspension units and a host of other upgrades that give the machine better cornering performance and rear wheel traction.

The front cowl is designed to be more aerodynamically efficient at higher speeds. Thus the reduction in wind resistance can make a big difference in lap times.

SPECIFICATIONS

Engine:	Liquid-cooled, four-stroke, inline, four-cylinder, DOHC, 16 valves
Bore x stroke:	76.0 x 55.0 mm
Displacement:	998cc
Fuel system:	Fuel injection 43 mm x 4
Ignition:	Digital
Exhaust:	4 - 2 -1 - 2.
Lubrication:	Forced, wet sump with oil cooler
Gearbox:	Six-speed
Clutch:	Wet, multi-disc
Primary drive:	Gear.
Final drive:	Chain
Frame:	Backbone/twin-tube, aluminium
Suspension	
Front:	43 mm inverted fork with top-out springs
Rear:	Bottom-Link Uni-Trak with gas-charged shock and top-out spring
Brakes	
Front:	Dual semi-floating 300 mm petal discs, dual radial-mount, opposed 4-piston, 4-pad
Rear:	Single 220 mm petal disc, single-bore pin-slide
Wheels	
Front:	17 in
Rear:	17 in
Tyres	
Front:	120/70ZR17M/C
Rear:	190/55ZR17M/C
Overall length:	2,065 mm
Overall width:	705 mm
Overall height:	1,130 mm
Seat height:	825 mm
Wheelbase:	1,390 mm
Dry weight:	175 kg
Tank capacity:	17 litres

The re-shaped rear end of the 10R has a clean and simple design. Brake/tail light and indicators sit neatly above the silencers.

An adjustable Öhlins steering damper with relief valve and twin-tube design is fitted as standard equipment.

Radial 4-pot opposed-piston callipers with 4 independent pads deliver impressive stopping performance with excellent feel at the lever.

Kawasaki Z1000 Naked

The story of the Z1000 starts back in 1972, when the company introduced the amazing Z1, a machine that was so good looking, it still attracts people today. It was initially destined to be introduced as a 750cc machine, but Honda spoilt the party by introducing their CB750. So Kawasaki decided to go one better and produced the more powerful and better equipped Z1. Now it was possible to own the biggest, most technically advanced and the fastest production machine in the world. This was a true superbike and would set the mould for many of the future Kawasaki machines.

Today, the new Z1000 is as lively and as modern as the Z1 was when it was introduced. Classic muscular styling gives it an aggressively angular look, and the latest technological advances make this machine a modern superbike to be ridden with respect. The increased low and mid-range torque allows better take-off acceleration in town, quicker corner exits when riding in the hills, and instantaneous acceleration when overtaking - just a few of the advances made on this awesome machine.

SPECIFICATION

Engine:	Liquid-cooled, four-stroke inline, four-cylinder, DOHC, 16 valves
Bore x stroke:	77.2 x 50.9 mm
Displacement:	953cc
Fuel system:	Carburettor fuel injection
Ignition:	Digital
Exhaust:	4 - 1 - 2. Quad style mufflers
Lubrication:	Forced, wet sump
Gearbox:	Six-speed
Clutch:	Wet, multi-disc
Primary drive:	Gear.
Final drive:	Sealed chain
Frame:	Tubular backbone (with engine sub-frame), high-tensile steel
Suspension	
Front:	41 mm inverted fork with stepless rebound damping and spring preload adjustability
Rear:	Bottom-Link Uni-Trak with gas-charged shock, stepless rebound damping and spring preload adjustability
Brakes	
Front:	Dual semi-floating 300 mm petal discs
Rear:	Single 250 mm petal disc
Wheels	
Front:	17 in
Rear:	17 in
Tyres	
Front:	120/70ZR17M/C (58W)
Rear:	190/50ZR17M/C (73W)
Overall length:	2,090 mm
Overall width:	780 mm
Overall height:	1,065 mm
Seat height:	820 mm
Wheelbase:	1,445 mm
Dry weight:	205 kg
Tank capacity:	18.5 litres

KTM Super Duke

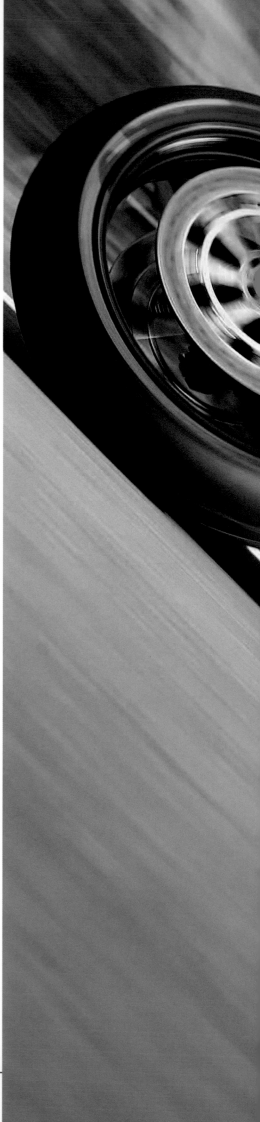

It continues to amaze me just how little people, away from the off-road scene, know about KTM. They are a well established company and since 1953 have captured more than ninety World Championship titles.

When the KTM 640 Duke, single cylinder model was presented back in 1994, people were amazed at what a fantastic machine that was. As development of the Duke series progressed, a new twin-cylinder unit - the KTM LC8 - was introduced, and the new road-going machine became the Super Duke. This was a whole new venture for the KTM Company, but the machine they produced is fast, fun and extremely competitive.

The Super Duke 990 is actually quite small in stature, and is only equipped with the essentials to help keep weight to a minimum. There is an alternative to the distinctive KTM orange colour, which is joined by all-black. The overall look of the machine is angular and although modern in style is not to everybody's taste, although the all-black paintwork gives it a slightly more aggressive characteristic.

The engine of the Super Duke, although large in capacity, is in fact very compact and very lightweight. It responds extremely quickly, and in conjunction with the stiff frame and well set-up suspension, the machine is a joy to ride, either at speed or in the city.

Alongside the standard Super Duke 990, a new 'R' model has also been introduced. This has been given a slightly more powerful engine and revised chassis, featuring numerous carbon-fibre and billet aluminium parts. It can be distinguished from its stablemate via its KTM-orange frame.

Neatly encased in the tubular chrome-moly space frame is the 75 degree, V-twin 999cc engine of the Super Duke.

Well laid-out instrumentation is essential on a machine like this. The bike has a mix of digital and analogue read-outs.

SPECIFICATION

Engine:	V-Twin, four-stroke, DOHC, liquid cooled
Bore and stroke:	101 x 62.4 mm
Displacement:	999cc
Fuel system:	Electronic injection
Ignition system:	Brakerless transistorised electronic ignition with digital ignition advance
Exhaust:	2 - 1 - 2, stainless steel silencer with catalytic converter
Lubrication:	Forced oil
Gearbox:	Six-speed
Clutch:	Multi-disc wet
Primary drive:	Straight tooth spur wheel
Final drive:	Chain
Frame:	Tubular chrome-moly space frame
Front suspension:	WP USD 48 mm
Rear suspension:	WP monoshock
Brakes	Brembo
Front:	320 mm discs, 2 x four-piston, fixed calliper
Rear:	40 mm disc, single-piston, floating brake calliper
Wheels	
Front:	3.5 x 17 in
Rear:	5.5 x 17 in
Tyres:	Pirelli Diablo
Front:	120 x 17 ZR 17 in
Rear:	180 x 55 ZR 17 in
Overall length:	2070 mm
Overall width:	810 mm
Overall height:	1100 mm
Seat height:	855 mm
Wheelbase:	1438 mm
Dry weight:	186 kg (without fuel)
Tank capacity:	18.5 litres

Twin stainless steel silencers with feed-back catalytic converter make their presence heard from under the rear seat.

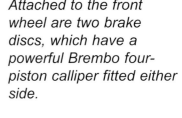

Attached to the front wheel are two brake discs, which have a powerful Brembo four-piston calliper fitted either side.

Moto Guzzi 1200 Sport

Moto Guzzi has made some pretty stunning machines over the past 85 years, but the 1200 Sport is something special. It keeps the traditional modern Moto Guzzi good looks, but also takes full advantage of the large 90° V-twin engine which works beautifully in conjunction with the ride setup.

The 1200 Sport model is a truly gritty 'naked' machine that also has incredible looks. The graphics are very distinctive and derive from the competition models, whilst the 'carbon fibre effect' silencer suggests speed, giving an immediate impression of the 1200 Sport's intentions.

Beautifully rounded styling and white racing plates either side of the rear tailpiece, turn the machine into an aggressive single-seater.

A baby fairing at the front is enough to confirm 'naked' status. This too has space for a racing number if required.

Beautifully finished and designed instrumentation gives the rider plenty of information.

SPECIFICATION

Engine:	90° V-Twin, four-stroke, air-cooled
Bore x stroke:	95 x 81.2 mm
Displacement:	1,151cc
Fuel system:	Fuel injection: Magneti Marelli IAW5A
Ignition:	2 x 45 mm throttle bodies, Weber IWP 162 injectors, Lambda control, twin spark ignition
Exhaust:	Stainless steel, 2 into 1 type with catalytic converter, height-adjustable muffler
Lubrication:	Splash
Gearbox:	Six-speed
Clutch:	Double disk, dry
Primary drive:	Helical teeth
Final drive:	Compact Reactive Shaft Drive CA.R.C.; double universal joint with floating bevel gear
Frame:	Tubular cradle, high tensile steel
Suspension	
Front:	Telescopic hydraulic fork with 45 mm and TIN surface treatment, preload adjustable
Rear:	Single arm suspension with progressive linkage, rear shock absorber adjustable in rebound and pre-load
Brakes	ABS Two channels, anti-block system
Front:	Twin stainless steel floating disc, wave type, Ø 320 mm, 4 opposed pistons
Rear:	Single steel fixed disc, Ø 282 mm, floating calliper with 2 parallel pistons
Wheels	Three spokes, light alloy, gravity die-casting
Front:	3.50 x 17 in
Rear:	5.50 x 17 in
Tyres	
Front:	120/70 ZR17 in
Rear:	180/55 ZR17 in
Overall length:	2195 mm
Overall width:	840 mm
Overall height:	1160 mm
Seat height:	800 mm
Wheelbase:	1.485 mm
Dry weight:	229 kg
Tank capacity:	23 litres

Fully adjustable 45mm forks help to enhance the handling, whilst Brembo brakes work tirelessly to slow the machine down.

Moto Guzzi MGS-01

The MGS-01 Corsa has proved to be competitive even from its first outing on 6th/7th March 2006, when rider Gianfranco Guareschi won the classic American race series 'Battle of the Twins' during the Daytona International Bike Week in Florida. Moto Guzzi MGS-01 and rider Guareschi followed up this incredible win with a further three victories and two second places, winning the national Supertwins title. Moto Guzzi could proudly say that they were back on the winning side of the track.

The fast-looking MGS-01 has a streamlined and feisty profile - compact mini-fairing, slim bodywork and neat rear-end. Cosworth pistons, chrome-plated cylinders and roller bearings, are just a few of the features that make the air-cooled, 1125cc, 90°, V-twin work so efficiently and reliably. Along with excellent weight distribution, race-designed rider position and the latest racing features, the MGS-01 is an exclusive motorbike built by craftsmen with the greatest of care and aimed at the true motorbike enthusiasts.

Each model is supplied with a book containing the rider's personal details, the frame number of the machine, and its cover and the stand carries the MGS-01 Corsa logo.

SPECIFICATION

Engine:	90° V-Twin, four-stroke, air-cooled, OHC, 4VPC	**Brakes**	
		Front:	Double floating disc, 320 mm, four pads, radial `callipers
Bore and stroke:	100 x 80 mm		
Displacement:	1,225cc		
Fuel system:	Marelli electronic fuel injection IAW 15M, digital. Marelli 50 mm throttle body	**Rear:**	Single disc, 220 mm, double piston calliper
		Wheels:	Forged aluminium, 5 spokes
Ignition system:	Electronic		
Exhaust:	2 into 1 Termignoni silencer	**Front:**	3.50 x 17 in
		Rear:	5.50 x 17 in
Lubrication:	Splash by pump lobe	**Tyres**	
Gearbox:	Six-speed	**Front:**	120/60 17 in Michelin slick S1246A
Clutch:	Sinterised double disc, dry		
Primary drive:	Straight-tooth gear	**Rear:**	180/55 17 in Michelin slick S1835A
Final drive:	Shaft with double universal joint		
		Overall length:	2,070 mm
Frame:	Rectangular section, single-beam ALS 450	**Overall width:**	730 mm
		Overall height:	1,165 mm
Front suspension:	Öhlins upside-down fork, 43 mm, 3 adjustment positions	**Seat height:**	820 mm
		Wheelbase:	1,450 mm
		Dry weight:	192 kg
Rear suspension:	Aluminium progressive swingarm with Öhlins monoshock absorber, four adjustment positions	**Tank capacity:**	18.5 litres
		Note: limited series non-homologated, for racing use.	

Moto Morini Corsaro 1200 Veloce

Moto Morini today is an independent industrial project that has made the decision to reclaim its place amongst the great Italian motorcycling brands of the day. The Moto Morini SpA shareholders are the Berti and Morini families, two important names in Bolognese manufacturing history. They are direct descendants of Alfonso Morini and the shareholders of Franco Morini Motori, a company that has been designing and building quality motorbike engines since 1954.

The new Moto Morini Company is founded on the desire to witness the comeback of one of the great names in Italian motorcycling. The challenges may be new and the technology the latest, but the founding values are the same as when Alfonso Morini established the company in 1937. Enter the Corsaro 1200 Veloce, a naked and aggressive machine born out of classic modern Italian styling and engineering.

The rear wheel supports a Pirelli Diablo tyre and the adjustment nut for taking up chain-slack is easily accessed within the swingarm casing.

The exhaust system has two slender, lightweight Termignoni silencers protruding from under the rear seat, which comply with Euro 3 emission standards.

The Corsaro 1200 Veloce uses the latest components and is equipped with up-to-the-moment technology. The name 'Veloce' translates into 'High Speed', and performance is what this machine is all about. This is a machine that will strike at the heart of any Italian motorcycle lover; it is created to give a rider ultimate fun and absolute performance. The engine is compact and well positioned, the trellis frame in high-strength tubular steel is extremely solid and combines all the stiffness required to harness the power of the Bialbero CorsaCorta V-twin engine. The Corsaro 1200 Veloce flaunts its gritty style aesthetically too, which can be seen in its graphics - the black technical base and monochromatic red upper structures accentuate the sporty character of this good-looking machine.

SPECIFICATION

Engine:	Bialbero CorsaCorta. 87° V twin-cylinder, four-valves, liquid cooling, DOHC
Bore x stroke:	107 x 66 mm
Displacement:	1187cc
Fuel system:	Magneti Marelli fuel injection, 54 mm throttle body
Ignition:	Magnetti Marelli, electronic
Exhaust:	Sport Termignoni with double silencer, 3-way catalytic converter and oxygen sensor
Lubrication:	Forced via trochoidal pump
Gearbox:	Six-speed
Clutch:	Multiplate in oil bath
Primary drive:	Chain
Final drive:	Chain
Frame:	ALS450 steel tubular trellis with varying diameters
Front suspension:	Marzocchi upside-down forks, with 50 mm/ 1.96 in stems
Rear suspension:	Single Sachs shock absorber. Aluminium swingarm
Brakes	Brembo
Front:	320 mm /12.59 in, double-disc with four-piston callipers
Rear:	220 mm / 8.66 in, single-disc with two-piston calliper
Wheels:	Brembo, light alloy, six-spokes
Tyres	Pirelli Diablo
Front:	120/70 ZR 17 in
Rear:	180/55 ZR 17 in
Overall length:	2070 mm
Overall width:	810 mm
Seat height:	830 mm / 32.67 in
Wheelbase:	1440 mm / 56.7 in
Dry weight:	196 kg (complete with battery, cooling liquid, engine oil - without fuel)
Tank capacity:	18 litres

The Gold Series Brembo brake systems delivers powerful yet progressive braking. Transmitting the sensitivity needed for optimum handling.

The heart of the Corsaro 1200 Veloce is the Bialbero CorsaCorta 1187cc twin cylinder engine. Its 87° V-layout is compact and full of character.

MTT Y2K Superbike

Located at the Port of West St. Mary, in Franklin, LA, USA, MTT has produced the ultimate in high performance machines - the MTT Turbine SUPERBIKE. The critically acclaimed SUPERBIKE is the world's first turbine-powered, street-legal motorcycle in its class, and has been recognised by Guinness World Records as the 'most powerful motorcycle ever to enter series production' and the 'most expensive production motorcycle'. Powered by a Rolls Royce Allison gas turbine engine, the SUPERBIKE has demonstrated over 300 hp and 425 ft/lb of torque on the Dyno Jet 200, and has been clocked at a record-breaking 227 mph.

The bike features a rear-mounted camera with LCD colour display, forward and rear-looking radar detector with laser scrambler, one touch 'Smart Start' ignition, and more. The MTT Turbine SUPERBIKE has starred in the Warner Brothers movie *Torque*, and Men's Journal lists the bike as one of the most 'awe-inspiring, innovative and otherwise amazing designs' in their feature article 'Perfect Stuff'.

Production is limited to five per year, so if you have the odd US$150,000, and you fancy this awesome machine in your garage, go to their website now!

SPECIFICATION

Engine:	Rolls Royce Allison 250 series gas turbine
Power:	320 hp @52,000 rpm (286 hp @ rear wheel)
Torque:	425 ft/lb @ 2,000 rpm
Output RPM:	6,000 rpm
Compressor Speed:	54,000 rpm
Fuel:	Diesel, kerosene
Lubrication:	Dry-sump/3.5quarts turbine oil
Gearbox:	Two-speed automatic
Frame:	Aluminium alloy
Fairings:	Carbon fibre
Suspension	
Shocks:	Mono-shock adjustable oleopneumatic, Öhlins
Front forks:	55 mm inverted
Brakes:	3 x 320 mm floating system - 4 piston callipers, Brembo
Wheels:	17 in carbon fibre, Dymag
Tyres	
Front:	120 60ZR17, Pirelli
Rear:	200 50ZR17, Pirelli
Rear View:	Rear-mounted camera with LCD colour display plus side mirrors

Seat:	Single or double
Colours:	Infinite custom colours
Seat height:	31.5 in
Wheelbase:	68 in
Weight:	500 lb
Tank capacity:	8.5 gallons (34 litres)

MV Agusta F4 Tamburini

I f you want one of the best-looking motorcycles in the world, and I am talking MV Agusta F4 Tamburini, you had better hurry and call MV. Three hundred only are being made and you may already be too late. Beware though, you need deep pockets, they do come at a price!

The F4 Tamburini was named after one of the most exciting Italian motorcycle designers ever. Massimo Tamburini was a co-founder of BiMoTa - his initials help to make up the company name. He is currently working at the CRC (Centro Ricerche Cagiva), a subsidiary of MV Agusta, but is credited with designing the Bimota DB1, Ducati Paso, Ducati 851, Ducati 888, the stupendous Ducati 916 and, yup you guessed it, the MV Agusta F4. What a CV!

When one talks about something being absolutely gorgeous, it's usually a male getting very hot under the collar about a female. But there are always exceptions to the rule and the MV Agusta F4 Tamburini is that exception, it is without doubt absolutely gorgeous! Designed by a genius, it has been given his name. It bristles with the latest technology and has to be one of the most exciting motorcycles on earth!

The F4 model was the machine that relaunched the MV company in 1988 and since then the company has not been without its troubles. Today though, it can boast an incredible array of machines of which the Limited Edition Tamburini is just one of those jewels in the crown.

The F4 is a unique and sought-after bike, with its four pipe undertail exhaust system, single-sided swingarm, large front forks (49 or 50 mm diameter) and traditional MV Agusta red and silver livery. The F4 is also one of the only production superbikes to have a cassette-style transmission and radial valved engine.

The engine was derived from the 1990-1992 Ferrari Formula One engine, with Ferrari engineers assisting in the early design and development stages. MV, although keeping the most important aspect of the engine - the radial valves - deviated from the Ferrari design. Today the F4 engine is unique in the sense that it is the only radial valved motorcycle engine currently in production.

The F4 1000 Tamburini is a creation in which MV President Claudio Castiglioni, celebrates the genius of the most famous designer in the field. A magical bike combining meticulous attention to detail and choice of the most exclusive components with an engine designed specifically to provide a thrilling performance.

The F4 Tamburini is a magical machine which combines meticulous attention to detail with a choice of the most exclusive components. This bike has an engine that was designed specifically to provide the most thrilling ride for its owner.

SPECIFICATION

Engine:	Four-cylinder, four-stroke, 16-valve, liquid cooled.
Bore x stroke:	76.2 x 55.9 mm.
Displacement:	996.33cc.
Fuel system:	Marelli Multipoint electronic injection.
Ignition:	Weber Marelli 16M.
Exhaust:	4 into 1 into 2 into 4.
Lubrication:	Wet sump.
Gearbox:	Six-speed, constant mesh, cassette-type.
Clutch:	Wet, multi-disc.
Primary drive:	Gear.
Final drive:	Chain.
Frame:	CrMo steel tubular trellis (TIG welded).
Front suspension:	Upside-down telescopic hydraulic fork, with rebound-compression damping and spring preload adjustment.
Rear suspension:	Progressive, single shock absorber with rebound and compression (high speed / low speed) damping and spring preload. Single-sided magnesium alloy swingarm.
Brakes	
Front:	Double steel floating disc 310 mm, six-piston calliper.
Rear:	Single steel disc 210 mm, four-piston calliper.
Wheel:	Forged aluminium alloy.
Front:	3.50 x 17 in.
Rear:	5.75 x 17 in.
Tyres	
Front:	120/65ZR 17 (56 W).
Rear:	180/55ZR 17 (73 W) or 190/50ZR 17 (73 W).
Overall length:	2007 mm.
Overall width:	685 mm.
Seat height:	809 mm.
Wheelbase:	407 mm.
Dry weight:	187 kg.
Tank capacity:	21 litres.

The intricate pathway of the exhaust system, seen here feeding into two silencers and finally turning into four small pipes that protrude from the rear.

With the power and speed produced by the F4, you would want to know that it could stop easily. That's why it has twin discs and six-piston callipers.

Instrumentation is a mix of digital and analogue and has an abundance of data that will keep the rider well informed of any problems.

MV Agusta Brutale 910R

The Brutale is a modern-looking machine with elegant lines. It transmits a powerful roar from the engine, and has exceptional performance. Even though it has been around for a few years, it has lost none of its charisma and has become a respected cult machine, oozing style and power.

Besides the standard models, 2007 has brought a one-off special to celebrate Italian success in the football World Cup. President of MV, Claudio Castiglioni, promised the Italian players and coach an MV Agusta Brutale 910R 'Italia', a special edition model of this most prestigious of motorcycles. It features a colour scheme based on the Italian flag and the team jersey - light blue bodywork and the word 'Italia' in gold. The words 'Campioni del Mondo 2006' will be featured on the fuel tank below a copy of the cup presented to the winners. Each of the machines presented to the individual team members will also bear the same number as his jersey and each will also have a small gold plate on the steering head bearing the player's name and number.

The same model will be manufactured in a limited edition of 100 and made available to MV Agusta collectors and enthusiasts.

You could say that the Brutale has elegant lines; it certainly has a powerful roar from the engine, and pretty amazing performance.

SPECIFICATION

Engine:	Four cylinder, four-stroke, 16-valve, liquid cooling, DOHC.
Bore x stroke:	76 x 50.1 mm.
Displacement:	909cc.
Fuel system:	Marelli Multipoint electronic injection.
Ignition:	Weber Marelli 5SM.
Exhaust:	4 into 1 into 2. One -piece system.
Lubrication:	Wet sump.
Gearbox:	Six speed, constant mesh, cassette type.
Clutch:	Wet, multi-disc.
Primary drive:	Gear.
Final drive:	Chain.
Frame:	CrMo steel tubular trellis (TIG welded).
Front suspension:	Upside-down telescopic hydraulic fork, with rebound-compression damping and spring preload adjustment.
Rear suspension:	Progressive, single shock absorber with rebound and compression (high speed / low speed) damping and spring preload. Single-sided aluminium alloy swingarm.
Brakes	
Front:	320 mm double floating discs with steel braking band and aluminium flange. Radial-type calliper with four pistons.
Rear:	210 mm single steel disc. Four piston calliper.
Wheels	Forged aluminium alloy.
Front:	3.50 x 17 in.
Rear:	6.00 x 17 in.
Tyres	
Front:	120/70ZR 17 (58 W).
Rear:	190/55ZR 17 (75 W).
Overall length:	2020 mm.
Overall width:	760 mm.
Seat height:	805 mm.
Wheelbase:	1410 mm.
Dry weight:	185 kg.
Fuel tank capacity:	19 litres.

The instrument cluster is very user-friendly and is equipped with all the necessary information.

The rear-end of the Brutale special edition 'Italia'. You wouldn't want to place a sticky racing number on this beautiful paintwork!

The number five shirt was worn by Fabio Cannavaro during the 2006 Football World cup. This therefore could be his machine!

Clearly demonstrated here is the single-sided swing-arm, and the chain final drive curling itself around the rear wheel sprocket.

NCR Macchia Nera

The NCR factory is located at Borgo Paginale, Italy. Yes, you may recognise that name - it's the home of Ducati motorcycles. NCR have been taking standard Ducati machines and turning them into world-beating racers since the 1960s. Now they have produced a stunning concept bike of their own.

How do you create such a piece of art, what are the ingredients and how do they all come together?

Well, take Stefano Poggipolini (President of the Poggipolini Group), put him together with his good friend Aldo Drudi (famed Italian designer), simmer for a while, allowing the free expressive aromas to come to the boil, and then gasp with amazement as the creation gels into a masterpiece of creative metallurgy.

Perhaps it was the Frankie Chili WSBK Ducati 998RS testastretta engine, poised prominently before them, that gave these men the idea of creating something really special. All the same the NCR craftsmen went immediately to work, building the full frame of gorgeous titanium to tightly encase the testastretta superbike engine. Using the finest materials of the day they followed Drudi's design to create the amazing Macchia Nera - Black Spot!

The first viewing of this amazing machine was at the Milan Motorcycle Exposition in 2003. Visitors flocked to the NCR stand and stood amazed and shocked at this incredible design, the ensemble of titanium, aluminium, magnesium and steel parts mixing with harmony and expression. The Macchia Nera concept bike is high-tech, and has great impact thanks to its aggressive Italian design - it's fast, brutally so, one hundred and eighty five horsepower fast!

2007 was to be the year when the Macchia Nera would finally be produced. It was said that it would be slightly heavier than the prototype and that it would have a headlight assembly. Whatever, this was a machine that all the Motorcycling Press and motorcycle enthusiasts around the world were waiting for. It would without doubt be amazing!

SPECIFICATION

(Note: Because this is a concept machine, it would be misleading to give figures that are not yet confirmed, and so these are marked as N/A)

Engine:	Ducati testastretta 998R
Bore x stroke:	N/A
Displacement:	N/A
Fuel system:	N/A
Ignition:	Electronic
Exhaust:	2 into 1 into 2
Lubrication:	N/A
Gearbox:	N/A
Clutch:	Anti-skid in Nipploy
Primary drive:	N/A
Final drive:	Chain with titanium sprockets.
Frame:	9 degree titanium frame (diameters 25/28/33 mm), weight 4.080 kg.
Rear	subframe in titanium
Front suspension:	Öhlins racing forks
Rear suspension:	Öhlins shock absorber
Brakes	Brembo racing.
Wheels	Marvic magnesium
Front:	3.50 x 16.5 in
Rear:	5.50 x 16.5 in
Tyres:	Dunlop intermediate racing tyres
Overall length:	N/A
Overall width:	N/A
Overall height:	N/A
Seat height:	N/A
Wheelbase:	N/A
Dry weight:	135 kg
Tank capacity:	N/A

SUZUKI GSX1400 FE

The original GSX1400 made its debut back in 2001 in Japan and 2002 in Europe, and just like today's version, it was a stunning machine with muscular looks and stunning performance.

Sadly the GSX1400 is on borrowed time and 2007 sees it celebrate its last year with a special edition model, the GSX1400 (FE) Final Edition. Strict Euro III emissions regulations currently in force have determined the future of this faithful machine - it is to be withdrawn from sale.

There is no doubting that it will always remain a favourite muscle-style machine, and the latest and last edition keeps up that reputation, featuring a Yoshimura dual cone exhaust system and limited edition graphics. Like a dinosaur that is about to become extinct, this machine will live on in the memories of those riders who got so much pleasure from its awesome power and good looks. It has and still does give its riders ultimate pleasure and exhilarating rides.

Classic retro style instruments in chrome, with the speedometer showing both mph and kph.

The rear suspension on the FE is a simple affair - coil springs with oil damping. Rear footpegs fold out when needed.

Giving away some of the FE's current secrets - behind this panel are the four carburettors that feed the four cylinders.

Shown is the rear wheel adjustment system, which also tightens/slackens the final-drive chain. A single brake disc and calliper is in the background.

SPECIFICATION

Engine:	Four stroke, four-cylinder, air-cooled with SACS, DOHC
Bore and stroke:	81.0 x 68.0 mm
Displacement:	1402cc
Fuel system:	Fuel injection
Ignition:	Electronic ignition (transistorised)
Exhaust:	4 into 1, Yoshimura dual cone
Lubrication:	Wet sump
Gearbox:	Six-speed constant mesh
Clutch:	Wet multi-plate
Primary drive:	Gear
Final drive:	Chain
Frame:	Double-cradle
Front suspension:	Telescopic, coil spring, oil damped
Rear suspension:	Swingarm type, coil spring, oil damped
Brakes	
Front:	Twin disc
Rear:	Single disc
Wheels	
Front:	17 M/C x MT 3.50
Rear:	17 M/C X MT 6.00
Tyres	
Front:	120/70ZR17 M/C (58W) tubeless
Rear:	190/50ZR17 M/C (73W) tubeless
Overall length:	2160 mm
Overall width:	810 mm
Overall height:	1140 mm
Seat height:	790 mm
Wheelbase:	1520 mm
Dry weight:	226 kg
Tank capacity:	22 litres

SUZUKI Hayabusa

The Suzuki GSX1300R, probably better known as the Hayabusa, is a hypersport motorcycle initially introduced in 1999, causing quite a stir amongst the motorcycle fraternity. The bike was consistently tested as the fastest production motorcycle in the world, until a detuning agreement was settled in 2001, which limited the top speed to 299 kph/186 mph.

Top speed today is a real problem, especially when you are trying to find out if a machine really can reach 320 kph (200 mph). German autobahns were usually the place to test these rockets, but even that can now be problematic due to traffic congestion. So if you want to see if the 'Busa will in fact reach that incredible top speed, it's probably best to believe what you read or get yourself onto the Bonneville Salt flats in Utah, USA.

There has always been some rivalry between Kawasaki and Suzuki when it comes to the title 'fastest production machine'. When Kawasaki presented their king of the road ZZR1400 hypa-bike, Suzuki, like a slick and confident poker player, quietly laid its cards on the table and presented their up-dated, up-rated and gorgeous-looking new 'Busa'......did I hear a disgruntled moaning sound!

The sleek lines and incredibly low drag co-efficiency of the new Hayabusa is, like the original machine, down to many hours spent in the wind tunnel, honing and shaving tiny bits from the bodywork to make it even more slippery. The results can clearly be seen in the new headlight, smoother contours of the fairing and the double-bubble windscreen, positioned a half-inch higher than before. With its extremely efficient aerodynamics, it will cut through the air like a hot knife through butter. Hang on for the ride of your life!

Welcome the 2008 Suzuki Hayabusa. The new machine delivers an entirely new level of balanced performance, redefining the ultimate sports class. It combines seemingly effortless acceleration, wind-cheating aerodynamics and a three-way selectable engine mapping to suit a rider's personal preference.

SPECIFICATION

Engine:	Four stroke, four-cylinder, liquid-cooled, DOHC
Bore and stroke:	81 mm x 65 mm
Displacement:	1340cc
Fuel system:	Fuel injection
Ignition:	Electronic ignition (transistorised)
Exhaust:	4 into 2. Lightweight aluminium silencers
Lubrication:	Wet sump
Gearbox:	Six-speed constant mesh
Clutch:	High-capacity clutch featuring back-torque limiter system
Primary drive:	Gear
Final drive:	Chain
Frame:	Rigid twin-spar, aluminium alloy
Front suspension:	Inverted telescopic, coil spring, spring preload fully adjustable
Rear suspension:	Link type, oil damped, coil spring, spring preload, fully adjustable
Brakes	
Front:	310 mm twin disc, radial mount, four-piston callipers
Rear:	260 mm disc, one-piston calliper
Wheels	Cast aluminium alloy
Front:	17 M/C x MT3.50
Rear:	17 M/C x MT6.00
Tyres	
Front:	120/70ZR17M/C (58W), tubeless
Rear:	190/50ZR17M/C (73W), tubeless
Overall length:	2195 mm
Overall width:	740 mm
Overall height:	1170 mm
Seat height:	805 mm
Wheelbase:	1485 mm
Dry weight:	220 kg
Tank capacity:	21 litres

No this isn't the flight-deck of the USS Enterprise, just the instrumentation for the 'Busa. Plenty to keep an eye on though!

With such high speeds being attained it's good to know the brakes are sufficient - twin discs with four-piston callipers.

More sculpted, more aerodynamic, better wind resistance. The front of the 'Busa has had further work done to help it cut through the wind more efficiently.

SUZUKI GSX-R1000

The GSX - R1000 model was introduced by Suzuki back in 2001, to replace the ageing GSX-R1100. Although smaller in capacity, the machine did more than make up for it in many other ways, going on to be one of the most popular sports motorcycles in the world. It also dominated on the race tracks, from where the road-going version gained much of its sporting make-up.

Over the years the GSX-R has become more refined, better looking and nicer to ride. For the 2007 model, there is a new 999cc engine with increased power, torque and acceleration. Forged aluminium alloy pistons, chrome-moly shotpeend connecting rods, hollow camshafts, and a secondary balancer shaft for reduced vibration are just a few of the improvements. A more compact fuel injection system featuring the Suzuki Dual Throttle Valve System (SDTV), for improved fuel delivery, is added along with many other smaller but significant changes.

Along with the new engine comes a new improved chassis too. This new aluminium alloy twin-spar frame is built using five castings for lightweight, incredible handling and performance, increased production precision, and reduced weight. At the same time the new braced aluminium alloy swingarm is more rigid and features an innovative new link system, which pivots on the swingarm itself for increased traction and reduced side loads. New forks and rear shock, along with a new electronically controlled steering damper and adjustable rider footpegs, all add up to rider satisfaction with safer and more comfortable riding.

With its wind tunnel developed bodywork featuring an aggressive new style and reduced frontal area, taller windscreen for optimum aerodynamic peformance, this is a bike that can slice through the air with ease and will give its owner a ride that they will want to return to again and again.

SPECIFICATION

Engine:	Four-stroke, four-cylinder, liquid-cooled, DOHC
Bore x stroke:	73.4 mm x 59 mm
Displacement:	999cc
Fuel system:	Fuel injection
Ignition:	Electronic ignition (transistorised).
Exhaust:	High volume Suzuki Advanced Exhaust System (SAES) with equal length head pipes, under engine chamber leading to two compact aluminium/titanium mufflers
Lubrication:	Wet sump
Gearbox:	Six-speed, constant mesh
Clutch:	Hydraulic, self-adjusting with back-torque limiter and rack and pinion operating system
Primary drive:	Gear
Final drive:	Chain
Frame:	Aluminium alloy twin-spar
Front suspension:	Inverted telescopic, coil spring, spring preload fully adjustable, rebound and compression damping force fully adjustable
Rear suspension:	Link type, oil damped, coil spring, spring preload fully adjustable, rebound and compression damping force fully adjustable
Brakes	
Front:	310 mm twin discs
Rear:	220 mm single disc, single-piston calliper
Wheels	Cast aluminium, three-spoke
Front:	17 M/C x MT 3.50
Rear:	17 M/C X MT 6.00
Tyres	Bridgestone
Front:	120/70-ZR17 in
Rear:	190/50-ZR17 in
Overall length:	2045 mm
Overall width:	720 mm
Overall height:	1130 mm
Seat height:	810 mm
Wheelbase:	1415 mm
Dry weight:	172 kg
Tank capacity:	18 litres

The racing idea that simpler is better is expressed in the vertically stacked, new shape headlamp, which gives a more compact projector beam

The exhaust mid-pipe carries an oxygen sensor, used by the engine management system to fine-tune the amount of fuel injected into the cylinders.

A new rear shock mounting system uses an aluminium-alloy link that pivots directly on the swingarm, with link rods connected to the frame.

TRIUMPH Rocket III

When introduced in 2004, the Rocket III not only astounded the general motorcycling world, but it also became a great success. A machine of this type was generally the territory of some insane engineer, working from his garden shed. This was no back-street animal, it was a well presented, beautifully finished, reliable and comfortable road-bike, that could be ridden with ease.

The Rocket III is a bike that isn't easily mistaken or missed. Built around a three-cylinder engine, tucked neatly under a huge fuel tank, this is what Americans would affectionately call a 'mother' of a machine. It's a bike with brute force and plenty of grunt - yet riding it couldn't be easier. The massive power of this machine is easily controlled and makes riding with a passenger a real joy.

It isn't that rare to see a Rocket III on the road; many have been sold and there is a well organised Rocket III club. The machine is very low-slung, with a low centre of gravity, helping to give a composed riding position, along with good balance and bike control. What is important with this huge monster is that the brakes work well and stopping is not a struggle. With its maintenance-free shaft drive, the awesome power from the 2.3 litre engine is transferred to the massive 240/50 section rear tyre without hesitation. Open that throttle and hang on as the revs pick up and the wind starts to whistle around your helmet.

Triumph have also given Rocket III owners masses of choice when it comes to personally customising and enhancing their bikes. Street-rodders can add exhaust pipes and a host of chrome parts, including engine dresser bars and side panels. For those who really want to impress, there are leather panniers that are constructed from the highest quality 4 mm aniline leather, and feature triple themed detailing and quick release chromed buckles.

Two big twin headlamps perch on the front of the Rocket III, giving plenty of night vision when needed.

The single disc and large 2-piston calliper help to slow this monster down and give good progressive control in the braking zone.

SPECIFICATION

Engine:	Liquid-cooled, DOHC, in-line three-cylinder
Bore x stroke:	101.6 x 94.3 mm
Displacement:	2294cc
Fuel system:	Multipoint sequential electronic fuel injection
Ignition:	Digital, inductive type via electronic engine management system
Exhaust:	3 into 1 into 3
Lubrication:	Wet sump
Gearbox:	Five-speed
Clutch:	Wet, multi-plate
Primary drive:	Gear
Final drive:	Shaft
Frame:	Tubular steel, twin spine
Front suspension:	43 mm upside-down forks
Rear suspension:	Chromed spring twin shocks with adjustable preload
Brakes	
Front:	Twin 320 mm floating discs, 4-piston callipers
Rear:	Single 316 mm disc, 2-piston calliper
Wheels	Alloy 5-spoke
Front:	17 x 3.5 in
Rear:	16 x 7.5 in
Tyres	
Front:	150/80 R 17
Rear:	240/50 R 16
Overall length:	2500 mm
Overall width:	970 mm (handlebars)
Overall height:	1165 mm
Seat height:	740 mm
Wheelbase:	1695 mm
Dry weight:	320 kg
Tank capacity:	24 litres

Nothing complicated about the instrumentation. Two smart chrome dials - speedometer on the left and tacho on the right.

The Rocket III Classic - a perfect bike for those lazy, long haul trips. Bars are high and pulled back and forward-set footboards are included.

TRIUMPH
Daytona 675

The Daytona 675 doesn't immediately shout 'superbike', but take a step closer and spend a little time to get to know it and you might be surprised. Yes, OK, it's only 675cc but that means nothing. The engine is without doubt nimble and powerful, but it's the whole package that you have to consider. This is a middleweight machine and looks and feels just as it should for that category of bike.

The 675 can deliver incredible performance from its compact and powerful water-cooled, three-cylinder, twelve-valve engine. Its sharply defined lines and under-seat exhaust system, all go to making this a great-looking machine that also has the power to thrill. It has truly earned the praise heaped upon it by some of the toughest critics in the motorcycle press, and has once again been named 'Bike of the Year' by *Masterbike* and *Supertest* in 2007.

Although the Daytona 675 was introduced in 2006, its development work started way back in 2000. Triumph had decided on a middleweight sport bike built to replace the Daytona 650, but unlike its predecessor it would be a three-cylinder model rather than the four cylinders, as used by the 650. Even before it hit the showrooms it gained praise from *BIKE* magazine, which pronounced it 'best British sportsbike ever' and possibly 'one of the greatest sportsbikes of all time'.

Rear suspension consists of piggyback reservoir shock, and the rear braking system has a single disc with single piston calliper.

A programmable gear change indicator illuminates seven LEDs to let you know the optimum point at which to change up, for maximum performance.

A well designed and shaped fairing all adds to the 675's good looks and aerodynamic efficiency.

The standard exhaust features an efficient underseat end-can and also utilises a secondary valve to boost torque low down.

The Daytona 675 has not only received global recognition for its performance on the road, but also for its outstanding ability on the race track. To follow this up Triumph have launched a new Racing Support Programme, which includes a new range of Triumph Genuine Race Parts, developed in-house and in collaboration with Paul Young Racing. These include a range of engine internals, such as revised cams, valve springs and valves, which are complemented by a new engine management unit and wiring harness, specifically designed with racing in mind. Also included is a transmission set, race air filter, a slipper clutch and many other track-focused parts.

SPECIFICATION

Engine:	Liquid-cooled, DOHC, in-line 3-cylinder
Bore x stroke:	74.0 x 52.3 mm
Displacement:	675cc
Fuel system:	Multipoint sequential electronic fuel injection with forced air induction
Ignition:	Digital, inductive type, via electronic engine management system
Exhaust:	3 into 1
Lubrication:	Wet sump
Gearbox:	Six-speed, close ratio
Clutch:	Wet, multi-plate
Primary drive:	Gear
Final drive:	Chain
Frame:	Aluminium beam twin spar
Front suspension:	41 mm USD forks with adjustable preload, rebound and compression damping
Rear suspension:	Monoshock with piggy back reservoir adjustable for preload, rebound and compression damping
Brakes	
Front:	Twin 308 mm floating discs, 4-piston radial callipers with radial master cylinder
Rear:	Single 220 mm disc, single piston calliper
Wheels	Alloy 5-spoke
Front:	17 x 3.5 in
Rear:	17 x 5.5 in
Tyres	Pirelli Super Corsa road/track compound
Front:	120/70 ZR 17
Rear:	180/55 ZR 17
Overall length:	2010 mm
Overall width:	710 mm (handlebars)
Overall height:	1109 mm
Seat height:	825 mm
Wheelbase:	1392 mm
Tank capacity:	17.4 litres

VINCENT
Black Lightning

Modern materials are cleverly used to create a new Vincent, whilst at the same time attention is paid to honour its past.

The adventure started when Howard Raymond Davies, a young British flying officer, was shot down and captured by the Germans in 1917. He dabbled with designs whilst in captivity and after the war, and less than ten years later in 1924, Davies and his partner E. J. Massey began building the HRD.

After some very successful years, sadly the company hit bad times and went into receivership. It was now that a young student, Philip Vincent, acquired the trademark, goodwill and few remaining HRD component parts for £500 (US$1000 approx).

Vincent continued to create and develop new machines between 1928 and 1955 when once again trouble hit with soaring debts. The company closed its doors and no more machines were manufactured. But even these events would not see the end of the Vincent.

Successful businessman, entrepreneur and lifelong motorcycle enthusiast Bernard Li acquired the trademarks, developed and negotiated alliances and manufactured the first prototypes of the new Vincent motorcycle, exhibiting four on October 4, 2002 in San Diego, USA. Careful design has seen the company recreate modern examples of those incredible machines, bringing the latest technology to a style that seems to be ageless - there is no mistaking the heritage of the Black Lightning S.

SPECIFICATIONS

Engine:	Liquid Cooled 90° V-Twin, DOHC, eight-valves
Bore x stroke:	100mm x 63.6mm
Displacement:	999cc
Fuel system:	Electronic Fuel Injection
Ignition:	Nippon denso digital electronic CDI
Exhaust:	2 into 2
Lubrication:	N/A
Gearbox:	Six Speed
Clutch:	Wet Multi-plate
Primary drive:	N/A
Final drive:	Chain
Frame:	Aluminium spine frame with tubular engine hangers
Front suspension:	43mm Showa telescopic forks
Rear suspension:	Tubular aluminium cantilever swingarm, Fox monoshock

Brakes	
Front:	Dual 320mm Brembo/4-piston calliper
Rear:	220mm Brembo/2-piston calliper
Wheels	
Front:	Forged 3.5 x 17"
Rear:	Forged 5.5 x 17"
Tyres	
Front:	120/70-17
Rear:	190/50-17
Overall length:	N/A
Overall width:	N/A
Overall height:	N/A
Seat height:	787 mm
Wheelbase:	1588 mm
Dry weight	185 kg dry
Seat height:	810 mm
Wheelbase:	1,418 mm
Tank capacity:	18 litres, 4 litre reserve

Clearly a leap forward here. Modern hi-tech instrumentation is used to keep the owner informed of the bikes performance.

The cooling radiator for the oil and two further radiators for the water hide the modern V-twin engine of the Lightning.

YAMAHA YZF R1

Designed to satisfy today's experienced supersport rider, the all-new Yamaha R1 is dynamic and exhilarating. The first generation R1 was introduced in 1988 and ever since that launch, each year people have wondered what Yamaha would do to improve an already superlative machine.

Once again Yamaha have taken their 'Art of Engineering' concept to create the new engine, chassis and bodywork, culminating in a remarkable new machine and reinforcing the company's position as a leading high-performance motorcycle manufacturer. This new fifth-generation R1 is packed with advanced new technology to keep its rider well informed, comfortably seated and ready for that all-inspiring, awesome ride.

The YZF-R1 is a legend of the supersport world, an acclaimed one-litre performer that's become a motorcycling icon, an all-powerful World Superbike race-winning machine that's also a monument to the power of beauty. The R1's performance is electrifying and yet what makes this motorcycle truly remarkable is its superb rider-friendly character - Yamaha's avant-garde, race-bred technology puts you confidently in control.

G.E.N.I.C.H. [Jenik] Genesis in Electronic engineering aimed at New, Innovative Control technology based on Human sensibilities. This is a rather long-winded explanation of Yamaha's dedication to man-machine interaction, and the technology they use to create the fusing of these two elements. Latest technology that will benefit the rider, and not just technology for technology's sake.

With the fifth-generation R1, Yamaha have also introduced YCC-I (Yamaha Chip Controlled Intake), the latest ground-breaking innovation in electronic intake control, designed to raise the already stunning performance of the new R1 to a new level.

With its all-new engine, chassis and bodywork, the new R1 has to be the most sophisticated, high-tech supersport machine built to date. It delivers the most exciting, rewarding and responsive riding experience you could ever want or imagine.

New radially-mounted, six-pot callipers grip the new smaller diameter discs, which are also thinner at their outer edge.

In order to enhance traction, the 2007 Z1 rear shock runs with revised compression damping settings, which offer a more progressive character.

Tucked behind the sculptured screen is a new instrumentation layout with a needle type tachometer and digital speedometer.

SPECIFICATION

Engine:	Liquid cooled, four-stroke, DOHC, four-valve, parallel four-cylinder
Bore x stroke:	77 x 53.6 mm
Displacement:	998cc
Fuel system:	Fuel injection
Ignition:	Digital TCI
Exhaust:	4 - 1 - 2
Lubrication:	Wet sump
Clutch type:	Wet multiple-disc, coil spring
Gearbox:	Six-speed, constant mesh
Primary drive:	Gear
Final drive:	Chain
Frame:	Aluminium die-cast Deltabox
Front suspension:	Telescopic forks
Rear suspension:	Swingarm
Brakes	
Front:	Dual discs, 310 mm
Rear:	Single disc, 220 mm
Wheels	
Front:	17 in
Rear:	17 in
Tyres	
Front:	120/70 ZR17MC (58W)
Rear:	190/50 ZR17MC (73W)
Overall length:	2,060 mm
Overall width:	720 mm
Overall height:	1,110 mm
Seat height:	835 mm
Wheelbase:	1,415 mm
Dry weight:	177 kg
Tank capacity:	18 litres (3.4 litres reserve)

YAMAHA XJR 1300

The XJ1300 has a history as long as your arm and a pedigree that any manufacturer would be proud of. It comes from a long line of well thought out machines that in their day have given so many riders so much pleasure and excitement. The latest 1300 is without doubt another example of an exhilaratingly fast and exceptionally comfortable machine that will thrill its rider.

The impressive four-cylinder engine pumps out more power than you will ever need - many people regard this machine as the ultimate 'Muscle' bike. There haven't been any wholesale changes from its predecessor, just subtle improvements adding to the gradual evolution of this legendary model. Whilst there have been changes, the overall character of the machine has remained steady.

The subtle range of engine and chassis changes are designed to ensure that this class-leading, naked Muscle bike continues to appeal to those riders who appreciate traditional style and serious performance, combined with up-to-the-minute technology. This latest version of the 1300 keeps its muscular looks and its sweet exhaust note, but has been given more torque, improved throttle response, top-of-the-range Öhlins shocks and re-profiled seat and handlebars for a more comfortable and exhilarating riding style.

The XJR's new fuel injection system has the same design as the sub-throttle system on the '04 model R1, and offers high levels of intake control.

A 4-2-1 exhaust system has an extremely high quality finish, underlining the XJR's enhanced performance and style

SPECIFICATION

Engine:	Air-cooled, four-stroke, four-valve, four-cylinder, DOHC
Bore x stroke:	79.0 x 63.8 mm
Displacement:	1,251cc
Fuel system:	Electric fuel injection
Ignition:	TCI
Exhaust:	4 into 2
Lubrication:	Wet sump
Gearbox:	Five-speed, constant mesh
Clutch:	Wet, multiple-disc coil spring
Primary drive:	Gear
Final drive:	Chain
Frame:	Steel, double cradle
Front suspension:	Telescopic fork
Rear suspension:	Swingarm with Öhlins shocks
Brakes	
Front:	Dual discs, 298 mm
Rear:	Single disc, 267 mm
Wheels	
Front:	17 in
Rear:	17 in
Tyres	
Front:	120/70 ZR17M/C (58W)
Rear:	180/55 ZR17M/C (73W)
Overall length:	2,175 mm
Overall width:	765 mm
Overall height:	1,115 mm
Seat height:	795 mm
Wheelbase:	1,500 mm
Dry weight:	222 kg
Tank capacity:	21 litres

YAMAHA YZF R6

L ike the R6 just wasn't a fabulous machine anyway, Yamaha keep adding to its list of improvements. Each year they find yet another little something to make the bike that bit better to ride and handle. The latest model features the MotoGP-derived YCC-T for ultra-precise throttle control, and aluminium Deltabox frame for intense cornering performance.

Over the years the R6 has benefited from an amazing array of racing hand-me-downs, and has become the most advanced production middleweight motorcycle Yamaha - or anybody else - has ever built.

Some of the latest features of the R6 are:

*   Quick-detach license plate holder and rear indicator mount, makes prepping for track days or racing easy.
*   Built-in lap timer controlled by a right-handlebar switch.
*   Multifunction digital and analog instrumentation features: programmable shift light, digital speedometer, analog tachometer, dual tripmeters with miles-on-reserve function, odometer, water temp guage and lights for neutral, high beam, low fuel and turn signals.
*   Standard tool kit is stored in a compartment under passenger seat.

SPECIFICATION

Engine type:	Liquid cooled, four-stroke, four-cylinder, 16-valves, D0HC
Bore x stroke:	67.0 x 42.5 mm
Displacement:	599cc
Fuel system:	Fuel injection
Ignition system:	TCI
Exhaust:	Midship muffler 4 into 1
Lubrication:	Wet sump
Gearbox:	Six-speed, constant mesh
Clutch:	Wet multiple-disc, coil spring
Primary drive:	Gear
Final drive:	Chain
Frame:	Aluminium die-cast Deltabox
Front suspension:	Telescopic fork
Rear suspension:	Swingarm
Brakes	
Front:	Dual discs, 310 mm
Rear:	Single disc, 220 mm
Wheels	
Front:	17 in
Rear:	17 in
Tyres	
Front:	120/70 ZR17M/C (58W)
Rear:	180/55 ZR17M/C (73W)
Overall length:	2,040 mm
Overall width:	700 mm
Overall height:	1,100 mm
Seat height:	850 mm
Wheelbase:	1,380 mm
Dry weight:	162 kg (with single seat 161 kg)
Tank capacity:	17.5 litres

YAMAHA MT-01

You only have to get a glimpse of the Yamaha MT-01 to see why it's such an exciting piece of machinery. You couldn't say it was good looking but it certainly has a mean streak to it, and its aggressive styling suits its manner right to the last nut and bolt. Whoever thought of putting a hi-tech 1,670cc V-twin engine into an aluminium sports frame, adding cutting-edge suspension and brakes, was without doubt having a great day at the office! This machine is desperate to take you where you want, as fast as you like and will handle the trickiest of situations with great courage.

The MT series was designed to shake up the streets with a whole new style of sports riding. Yamaha call it Torque Sports and it's all about uniting big-piston engines with sports chassis for a dramatic new riding experience. The Torque Sport roadsters perform to a different kind of beat, like Japan's legendary Kodo drumbeat, an earth-trembling expression of awesome latent power produced by massive bass drums.

Experience what Yamaha call Soul Beat - to really appreciate what Yamaha has created in the MT-01 it is important to understand the meaning of the central concept that guided its development project. In a word, that concept is a Soul Beat V-twin Sports. This beat in Japanese is KODO, a word that is used both for the beat of the human heart and the beat of drums.

The beat of drums or music is one of the most exciting and inspiring things human beings create. It touches our very souls and can move us quite dramatically and that is the kind of soul beat that Yamaha has built into the MT-01. It transmits every beat of its heart, allowing you to discover and enjoy the beat of that huge displacement V-twin's torque, making you feel like you are riding the engine itself.

This is not just a mean-looking, fast machine - it also has a soul, and only by riding it can you truly appreciate what Yamaha have produced in this extraordinary motorcycle.

Although the MT already looks radical, Yamaha can give it that extra edge to make your machine look even more exciting with a range of easy-to-fit styling accessories, including fly screen and carbon-fibre air intake scoops. If you're planning to personalise your MT-01 to the max, you'll want the single-seat kit and carbon heat shields that fit with the exhausts. A Stage one easy-to-fit, street-legal titanium Akraprovi silencer kit will make your MT-01 sound better, look better and feel better. Stage two and three accessories are strictly for track lovers.

The MT-01 looks pretty radical and retains much of the looks it had when shown for the first time. There is nothing delicate about it and the noise it produces sends a shiver down your spine.

The two massive silencers tuck neatly under the comfortable seat. Lack of long-distance styling leaves it void of the usual comforts for long-haul rides.

The power plant for the MT-01 is a slow-revving, push-rod, V-twin and is derived from the Road Warrior custom motorcycle.

The instrumentation is pure and simple and easy to read. Would you need anything else one wonders!

SPECIFICATION

Engine:	Air-cooled, 4-stroke, V-twin, OHV, 4-vpc
Bore x stroke:	97.0 x 113.0 mm
Displacement:	1,670cc
Fuel system:	Fuel injection
Ignition:	TCI
Exhaust:	2 into 1 into 2
Lubrication:	Dry sump
Gearbox:	Five-speed
Clutch:	Wet, multiple-disc
Primary drive:	Gear
Final drive:	Chain
Frame:	Aluminium CF die-cast, double cradle
Front suspension:	Telescopic forks
Rear suspension:	Swing arm. Link suspension
Brakes	
Front:	310 mm dual floating discs
Rear:	267 mm single floating disc
Wheels	
Front:	17 in
Rear:	17 in
Tyres	
Front:	120/70 ZR17 M/C (58W)
Rear:	190/50 ZR17 M/C (73W)
Overall length:	2,185 mm
Overall width:	800 mm
Overall height:	1,105 mm
Seat height:	825 mm
Wheelbase:	1,525 mm
Dry weight:	243 kg
Tank capacity:	15 litres

INDEX

Ackowledgements

The Publisher and Author would like to thank the following people and organisations for their kind help and input:

Aprilia UK; Benelli Q.J. s.r.l Pesaro, Italy; Bimota, Rimini, Italy; BMW UK; Daimlerchrysler, USA; Ducati Corse, Italy; Ducati UK Ltd., Milton Keynes, UK; Honda UK; Kawasaki UK; KTM-Sportmotorcycle UK Ltd; Moto Morini, Italy; Moto Guzzi, Italy; MTT (Marine Turbine), Franklin, LA, USA; MV Agusta Motorcycles S.p.A. Varese, Italy; NCR s.r.l Italy; Suzuki UK; Triumph Motorcycles, Leicester, UK; Yamaha Motorcycles, Weybridge, UK; Vincent Motors, San Diego, CA, USA; Speedaway Motorcycles, Warley, Birmingham, UK; Clarks Motorcycles, Rednal, Birmingham, UK; Windy Corner Motorcycles, Barwell, Leicester, UK; Wylie & Holland Motorcycles, Wellington, UK; KCS Group, Corby, Northants, UK; Rockingham Race Circuit, Corby, Northants, UK.

Note from the Author:

Please note that specifications are correct at the time of writing, but these can vary at anytime. For example, figures may vary according to the sales areas around the world, due to the changing regulations found in other countries.